INDIANS, INUIT, and MÉTIS

of Canada

Hope MacLean

gage PUBLISHING LIMITED
TORONTO ONTARIO CANADA

Illustrations by B.L. Plevan
Design by Susan Weiss
Cover design by Jean Galt
Photographs by Barry Griffiths
Assembly by Keith Murray

Acknowledgements

I would like to thank the many people, Native and non-Native, who gave their time to review this text. Their perceptive comments have led to many positive changes. I would also like to thank the artist, B.L. Plevan, whose delicate drawings enrich the text. Finally, I would like to thank my editors at Gage Publishing Limited, Jamie Smith, Gary Kenny, and Gordon Cluett, whose high standards kept me on my toes.
Hope MacLean

ISBN 0-7715-**8377-X**

2 3 4 5 6 7   JD   86 85 84 83

Written, Printed, and Bound in Canada

Table of Contents

Introduction iv

Chapter 1: The First People 1

    Canada's Regions 6

    Language Families 8

Chapter 2: The Micmac of the Atlantic Coast Region 13

    The Micmac Meet Europeans 20

Chapter 3: The Huron of the Great Lakes Region 27

    The Huron Meet Europeans 34

Chapter 4: The Ojibwa of the Northern Forest Region 39

    The Ojibwa Meet Europeans 46

Chapter 5: The Blackfoot of the Prairie Region 51

    The Blackfoot Meet Europeans 61

Chapter 6: The Haida of the Pacific Region 65

    The Haida Meet Europeans 74

Chapter 7: The Inuit of the Arctic Region 77

    The Inuit Meet Europeans 87

Chapter 8: The Métis 91

    The Riel "Rebellions" 97

Chapter 9: Contact With Europeans 103

    The First European Visitors 104

    Sudden Changes in Indian Life 109

    The Making of Treaties 110

Chapter 10: Modern Issues 117

    Native People and the Land 119

    Native Culture: Continuity and Change 123

    Organizing for the Future 128

Important Dates 131

Bibliography 134

Index 136

Introduction

Indians, Inuit, and Métis of Canada is a supplementary reference book about Canada's Native people — their past, present, and future. Its chief aim is to help students at the junior and intermediate levels gain a better understanding and appreciation of Native lifestyles and cultures.

Many books about Native people present them only from a European point of view. Native culture — the way Natives think and live — is often described as a collection of strange and odd customs. Little is written about the activities of Native people during the 500 years since the coming of Europeans. What activities are mentioned are usually tied to European activities. For example, how Indians guided explorers or how they showed settlers a cure for scurvy. Their own achievements are seldom recognized. And their modern concerns, lifestyles, and successes, too, are rarely mentioned.

Indians, Inuit, and Métis of Canada offers a view of the other side of Native life: why Native people lived the way they did; how the various aspects of Native culture fitted together to form a meaningful way of life; how the coming of Europeans changed that way of life; what Native people did about the changes; and what their life is like today.

While there are some reference books that do these things, most are written above the reading and comprehension levels of junior and intermediate students. This book, however, is written with such an audience in mind. Topics are discussed in a simple and logical manner. This is not to say that the book is written exclusively for junior and intermediate students. Indeed, senior students and adults, too, will find the book interesting and informative.

The specific goals of the book can be stated as follows:

- To encourage an understanding of the diversity of Native cultures. Native people were not, and are not, all the same. Even though television and movies, with their sometimes stereotyped portrayal of the Indian warrior wearing feathers and buckskin, might lead us to think so. In reality, Native people had many different ways of life.

- To show how the differences between groups of Native people were often the result of the land in which they lived. Canada is made up of a variety of landscapes — the rocky Atlantic shores, the wide belts of northern forest, the fertile fields of the Great Lakes area, the flat prairie, the great mountains of the Pacific, and the open stretches of tundra in the Arctic. Native people lived in each of these areas and adapted their lifestyles to the land and its resources.

- To show that these distinct nations were linked by a common respect for the land and the animals. Native people believed that animals were endowed with spirits, and must be respected. The land, too, received their respect, as it was the source of everything that they needed. As the Inuit say, "The land is our life."

- To show the effects that the coming of Europeans had on Native culture. The spiritual beliefs, lifestyles, politics, and education of Native people underwent tremendous changes in a relatively short period of time.

- To show the present day concerns of Canada's Native people. These include laws and government, treaties, land claims, and cultural survival. A knowledge of such concerns will enable the reader to understand Native issues better as they are encountered in newspapers, magazines, or on television.

To accomplish these goals, five Indian nations — the Micmac, the Huron, the Ojibwa, the Blackfoot, and the Haida — plus the Inuit have been selected for study. Each of these groups lived in one of Canada's six geographical regions. In many ways, they represent all the Native people who lived in each of these regions.

Particular topics are discussed, too. For example, language among the Micmac, kinship among the Haida, and sharing among the Inuit.

Finally, a number of features and graphic aids supplement the text. They include Native legends, biographies, and anecdotes; marginal notes; easy-to-read maps; and many distinctive drawings by Toronto artist B. L. Plevan. A time-line of dates used in the text, a bibliography, and an index have also been included for reference purposes.

1 The First People

Once in the long, long ago, there were two huge animals. One was a giant toad. The other was a beast with a horn on its head. The toad kept all the water in its body. It only let out a little bit at a time to moisten the earth.

One day, the two animals had a fight. The horned beast stabbed the toad in the side with its horn. The toad's body burst, and all the water flooded out over the earth.

Nanabush, who was part man and part god, saw the water coming. He snatched up all the animals he could find and rushed to the top of a mountain. There, he built a raft.

Soon the water rose above the top of the mountain. All the animals drowned except those that were on the raft with Nanabush.

Nanabush decided to make a new world. But with what? Maybe if he could get some of the mud lying under the water he could make a start. He called on all the animals that knew how to swim and asked them to try to reach the bottom.

First went the loon. It came back with nothing in its bill. Then, the otter and the beaver tried. They, too, failed. Finally, the little muskrat dived in. It stayed under the water for a long time. When it finally came up, it was dead. But clutched in its paws was some precious mud.

Nanabush blew on the still, wet muskrat and it came back to life. Then he rubbed the mud between his hands and blew on it. It spread across the water until at last there was land farther than the eye could see. Nanabush had made a new world.

Nanabush then journeyed across the new world. As he travelled, he created the Indian nations. He put each in a different part of the land and gave them their own religions, customs, and manners. And that is how the people came to be.

*   *   *

This is an Ojibwa story of how the earth and the people were created. Other Indian nations tell similar stories.

While these stories tell how Indians first came to North America, they do not tell when they came or where they came from. Some people believe that Indians have always lived in North America. Others believe that the Indians first lived somewhere else. Archaeologists, for example, have found many bones and skulls belonging to early forms of humans in Europe, Asia, and Africa. But they have found no such evidence in North America. Therefore, they conclude, Indians must have come to North America from other lands.

Archaeologists are people who uncover the remains of former civilizations to find out how people lived long ago.

There have been many theories or ideas about the first home of the Indian peoples. The most common one among archaeologists is that they came from Asia in the distant past, possibly as long ago as 30 000 years. Once, so the theory says, Asia and America were joined by a wide strip of land. Look at the map on the next page. You can see where the land bridge was. Even today, Asia and America are separated by a channel of water that is only ninety kilometres wide.

This channel is now called Bering Strait.

The land bridge was probably formed 65 000 years ago during the most recent Ice Age. Water from the ocean froze into huge sheets of ice called glaciers. So much water froze that it lowered the oceans by 100 m. Since the Bering Strait was less than 100 m deep, the seabed was exposed. This left a plain of dry grassy land almost 1600 km wide between the two continents. According to the theory, the ancestors of Indians came across the land bridge into North America. The crossings went on from time to time over many years.

What led people in Asia to cross into North America? Herds of animals travelled back and forth across the bridge, grazing as they went. Hunters and their families naturally followed the herds into North America, since the animals were their source of food. In this way, they gradually spread south and east over the continent. Once in North America, the people continued to live by hunting game. They moved around the plains covering the centre of the continent. This area is now known as the western United States.

In those days, the plains were not as dry as they are now. They were meadows of tall grass. Large animals roamed the plains, grazing on the grass. One of these was the mammoth, a huge elephant-like creature. Another was the big-horned bison, an early type of buffalo.

Archaeologists think that the first people in North America came from Asia. They probably moved south to the grasslands east of the Rocky Mountains, as the arrows on the map show. They may also have lived on the coastal plains in the Yukon Territory. Glaciers never covered this area. Archaeologists have found signs of early settlement there. ———————▶

THE PEOPLING OF NORTH AMERICA: POSSIBLE ROUTES

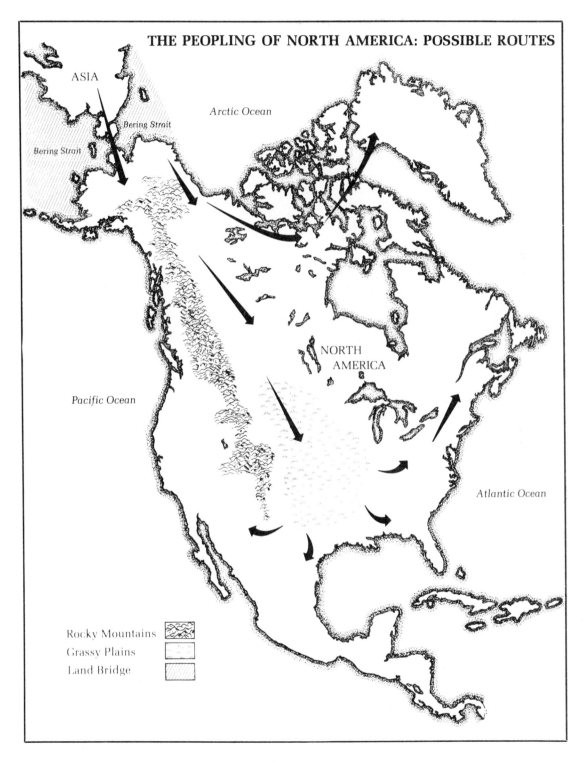

ASIA

Bering Strait

Bering Strait

Arctic Ocean

NORTH
AMERICA

Pacific Ocean

Atlantic Ocean

Rocky Mountains
Grassy Plains
Land Bridge

Indians hunted these animals with spears. They chipped the knife-sharp points of their spears from flint stones. Today, archaeologists find many bones of the animals the Indians hunted and killed. Sometimes, spear points are still lodged between the bones.

About 8000 B.C., the climate changed again. The ice covering much of what is now Canada began to melt. As a result, the ocean rose, flooding the land bridge. The plains became hotter and drier, and the plant life died. With their food gone, many animals began to disappear. In time, the largest animal left on the plains was the modern-day bison or buffalo.

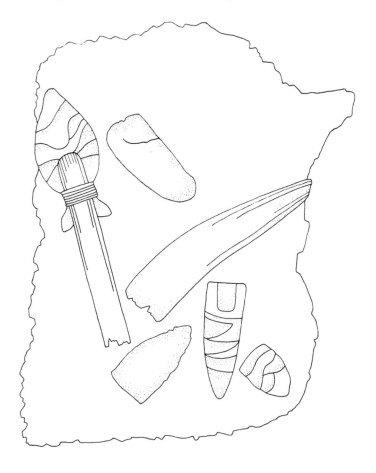

For hunting, Indians chipped spear points that looked like these. The curved object in the centre of the illustration is a bison rib. Today, archaeologists often find Indian spear points among the bony remains of animals such as bison.

A big-horned bison. These large animals once roamed the great plains of North America.

Once the ice had melted, some Indians began to move north into different parts of Canada. As they spread out, they formed groups called nations or tribes. Each had its own special habits and customs, its own culture.

Culture is the name given to the way in which a particular group of people live. It includes many things. It is how people think and behave. It is how they make their homes and their clothes. It is their language and their stories, their songs and their dances. It is their religion and their laws.

Many Indian nations, although they each had their own culture, had many habits and customs in common. For example, many hunted and fished in the same way. What was the reason for these common traits? They were probably the result of many groups living in a particular region and interacting with nature in a similar way.

A region is an area of land where the climate, the soil, and the kinds of animals and plants, are the same throughout. As you read this book, notice how the Indian nations developed ways of living suitable to the regions in which they lived.

Canada's Regions

There are six main regions in Canada. If you look at the map of regions, you can see where they are.

The largest region ranges across Canada from Labrador in the east to the Yukon Territory in the west. It is called the *northern forest*. The land has many softwood forests, with thousands of lakes and rivers. Indians hunted moose, deer, caribou, rabbit, porcupine, and beaver in the forests. And they caught trout, whitefish, pickerel, and perch in the lakes and rivers.

The people of the northern forest were nomads. They moved around most of the time. They had to move because the animals, fish, and plants they lived on were found in different places at different times of the year. To make travel easier, they built portable houses and used canoes, snowshoes, and toboggans.

There were nineteen Indian nations living in the northern forest. Seven of them lived from Labrador in the east to Alberta in the west. They were the Montagnais, Naskapi, Abenakis, Ottawa, Algonkin, Ojibwa, and Cree.

The other twelve nations lived farther north, mainly in the Northwest Territories and the Yukon Territory. They were the Sekani, Chipewyan, Yellowknife, Slavey, Dogrib, Hare, Nahani, Beaver, Loucheux, Tutchone, Han, and Kaska.

A second region is the *Atlantic coast*. It includes the provinces of Nova Scotia, New Brunswick, Prince Edward Island, and Newfoundland, as well as the Gaspé Peninsula part of Quebec.

The people of the Atlantic coast were the Beothuk, Micmac, and Malecite. They had many customs in common with the people of the northern forest. But there were also some differences. Because they lived close to the ocean, they ate seafood for most of the year. They preserved and stored this food to carry them over the lean times in winter.

A third region is found in southern Ontario and along the St. Lawrence River. It is called the *Great Lakes* region. The Indians here had a different way of using the land. They did not need to travel and hunt all the time. They were farmers.

The farmers of the Great Lakes region lived in large villages. They cleared the forests to grow such crops as corn, beans, squash, and tobacco. There were four nations of farmers: the Huron, Tobacco Huron, Neutral, and Iroquois.

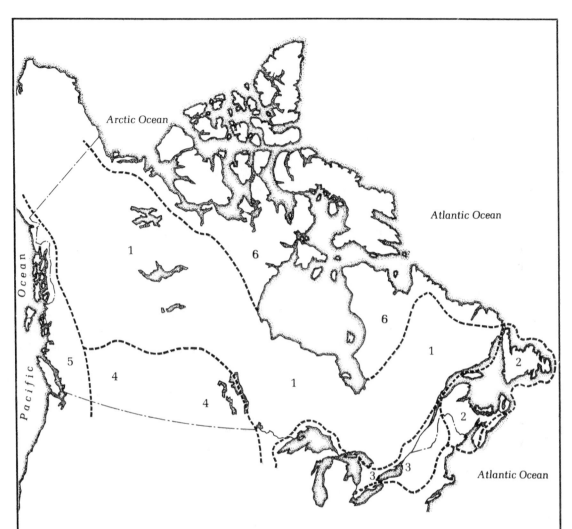

THE SIX REGIONS OF CANADA

1. Northern Forest   4. Prairie

2. Atlantic Coast   5. Pacific

3. Great Lakes   6. Arctic

The sizes of Canada's six regions vary greatly. Notice the vast amount of land taken in by the Northern Forest Region, and the small amount taken in by the Great Lakes Region.

A fourth region covers the southern parts of Alberta, Saskatchewan, and Manitoba. It is called the *prairies*. The land here is rolling grassland. It is ideal for grazing and once fed huge herds of woolly brown buffalo.

The prairie Indians lived by hunting the buffalo. So, like the people of the northern forest, they were always on the move. They lived in skin tents called tipis, which were easy to carry. They used dogs and, later, horses to help them move their household goods.

The Blackfoot nation was formed by a group of tribes, the Blackfoot, Blood, and Piegan.

The prairie people were the Assiniboine or Stony, Plains Cree, Blackfoot, Sarcee, Saulteaux or Plains Ojibwa, and Gros Ventre.

A fifth region includes the mountains, the coast, and the islands of British Columbia. It is called the *Pacific region*. The land is mountainous, with deep heavily-wooded valleys and fast-flowing rivers. Every year, millions of salmon swim up the rivers to breed.

Most of the Indians who lived in this region depended on the salmon. It could be dried and stored and was a constant source of food. This meant that the Pacific Indians did not need to travel all the time to find food. Most of them were able to live in permanent villages.

The Pacific Indians also hunted deer, elk, mountain goats, and sheep. Those who lived along the coast or on the islands hunted such sea-mammals as whales and sea lions.

The Indians of the Pacific region were the Haida, Tsimshian, Kwakiutl, Nootka, Interior and Coast Salish, Bella Coola, Tlingit, Kootenay, Chilcotin, Carrier, Tsetsaut, and Tahltan.

The tree line is the boundary beyond which it is too cold for trees to grow.

The sixth region includes all of Canada north of the tree line. It stretches from Labrador in the east to the Yukon Territory in the west. It is called the *Arctic region*. The people of the Arctic are the Inuit.

Most of the Inuit lived along the sea coast. Some lived on northern islands. They specialized in hunting such sea-mammals as seals, whales, and walrus. In summer, they moved inland to hunt caribou. The Inuit invented many clever tools which they carved from wood, bone, and stone.

Language Families

Besides grouping Indians according to regions, we can also group them according to language families. A language family is a group of related languages. Scientists believe that the languages in a family were once a single language. Why do they believe this? They have found similarities between languages that otherwise appear to be completely different.

Take English and French, for example. They are different languages. A French-speaking person and an English-speaking person can't understand one another. Yet the grammar and many words in these two languages are similar. Therefore, scientists conclude, they must have come from a single ancestral language.

How did a single language become many languages? According to the scientists, as groups of people spread out over many hundreds of years, the languages they spoke gradually changed.

There were eleven Native language families in Canada. Most of them were made up of many related languages. The Cree, Ojibwa, and Blackfoot nations, for example, belonged to the same language family.

LANGUAGE FAMILIES OF INDIANS AND INUIT

Algonkian
Abenaki
Algonkin
Blackfoot
Cree
Delaware
Malecite
Micmac
Montagnais
Naskapi
Ojibwa
Ottawa
Potawatomi

Athapaskan
Beaver
Carrier
Chilcotin
Chipewyan
Dogrib
Hare
Loucheux
Nahani
Sarcee
Sekani
Slave
Tahltan
Yellowknife

Eskimo-Aleut
Inuktitut

Haidan
Haida

Iroquoian
Cayuga
Huron
Mohawk
Oneida
Onondaga
Seneca
Tuscarora

Kootenayan
Kootenay

Salishan
Bella Coola
Comox
Cowichan
Lillooet
Ntlakyapamuk
Okanagan
Puntlatch
Seechelt
Semiahmoo
Shuswap
Songish
Squamish

Siouan
Assiniboine
Dakota
Sioux

Tlingit
Tagish

Tsimshian
Gitksan
Niska
Tsimshian

Wakashan
Haisla
Heiltsuk
Kwakiutl
Nootka

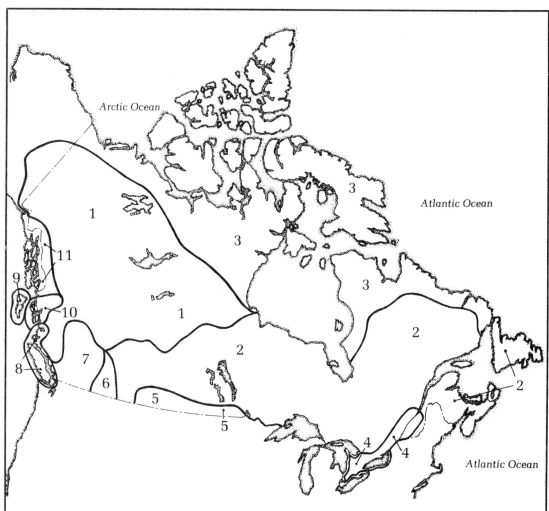

Arctic Ocean

Atlantic Ocean

Atlantic Ocean

LANGUAGE FAMILIES OF INDIANS AND INUIT

1. Athapaskan
2. Algonkian
3. Eskimo-Aleut
4. Iroquoian
5. Siouan
6. Kootenayan
7. Salishan
8. Wakashan
9. Haidan
10. Tsimshian
11. Tlingit

This map shows the general locations of Indian and Inuit language families.

Some Indian language families were widespread. The two largest were the Algonkian and the Athapaskan. They were spoken across nine-tenths of Canada (excluding the Arctic), and in several regions. Algonkian languages, for example, were spoken in the Atlantic coast region, the northern forest region, and the prairie region.

The Pacific region, however, was a different story. Seven different language families lived in one area. Why so many? One theory is that the mountains made it difficult for people to move farther inland. So when other groups came, speaking a different language, the people who were already there simply had to move over and give them room.

Look at the map of language families. Notice how some were widespread and how some covered only a small area.

The Indians and Inuit lived across Canada, from coast to coast to coast. In the following pages, we will look at six different nations, one in each of Canada's six regions. We will study the geography, the climate, the food, and other resources of each region. And we will study how the people interacted with the land and its resources to develop distinct cultures.

2 The Micmac of the Atlantic Coast Region

On the eastern shores of Canada, the Atlantic Ocean washes against rocky cliffs and beaches of pebbles, rock, and sand. Much of the land is island or peninsula. The long coastline curves around many bays and inlets. People who live here are never very far from the ocean.

The summers are mild because of the cooling breeze from the sea. The winters are not very cold, but the wind can be harsh. Cold winds from the east blow across the Atlantic, picking up speed, and sweep over the low-lying coasts. Only the inland forests offer some protection from the cold, damp winds.

This region is called the *Atlantic coast.* It includes the provinces of Nova Scotia, New Brunswick, Prince Edward Island, and Newfoundland, as well as the Gaspé Peninsula part of Quebec.

The people of the Atlantic coast were the Micmac and the Malecite. There was also a third people, the Beothuk, who lived in Newfoundland. There are no Beothuk today. Some were killed by Europeans or other Indians. Many died of epidemic diseases. The last known Beothuk, a woman named Shananditti, died in 1829.

The Micmac were the largest group. They lived throughout the Atlantic coast region. The Malecite, a smaller group, lived in the western part of what today is called New Brunswick. In this chapter, we will study the Micmac.

*　　*　　*

The Micmac were part of the great Algonkian language family, which spread as far west as the Rocky Mountains. How they got the name "Micmac" is a mystery. It may have come from the Malecite word *Mi k'am*, meaning "wood spirit." Their own name for themselves is *El'nu*, "the people."

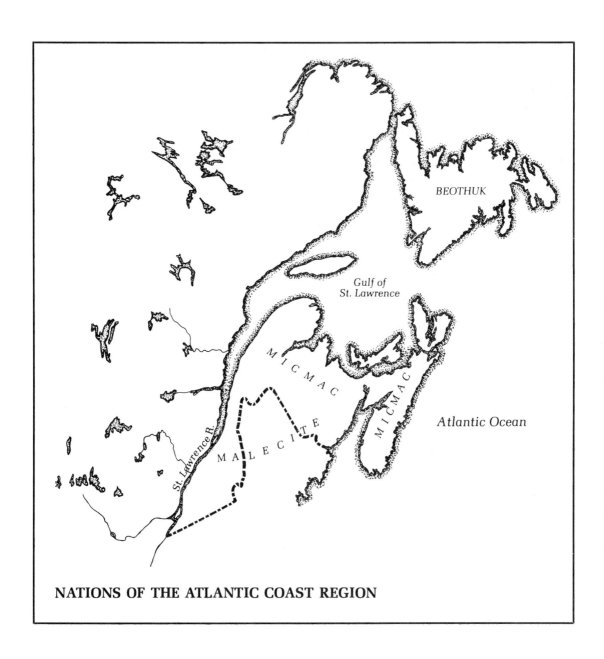

NATIONS OF THE ATLANTIC COAST REGION

Exactly when the Micmac came to the Atlantic coast region is not certain. One of the earliest signs of people living in the area is at Camp Debert in Nova Scotia. There, archaeologists found a hunting camp which they believe had been used as early as 8600 B.C. Scientists believe that during the last ice age, the land here was completely covered by ice. Ancestors of the Micmac may have moved in when the ice began to melt. The archaeologists suggest that Indians may have been using the camp when the ice sheets were only about 100 km away.

Where the Micmac came from is also a mystery. Their own legends say that they came from a land farther west.

The Micmac were fortunate in their choice of home. The waters surrounding their land are some of the richest fishing grounds in the world. One reason for this is the ocean currents. Off the Atlantic coast, the warm water of the Gulf Stream meets and mingles with cold water moving south from the Arctic. Where the two currents meet, they stir up minerals and nutrients from the shallow sea floor. Tiny creatures called plankton — so small that up to five million live in a litre of water — feed on the nutrients. The plankton, in turn, provides food for many shellfish. It also provides food for such fish as cod, mackerel, herring, and shad, which migrate to the Atlantic coast to breed. Flocks of sea birds and ocean mammals — seals, whales, and porpoises — follow, to feed on the masses of spawning fish, and to breed as well.

Nutrients are food materials that provide nourishment for the body.

For most of the year, the Micmac could depend on the nearby ocean for their food. Only in February and March, when fish migrated from the coast, did the Micmac face a serious food shortage. The resources of the land were not as rich and reliable as those of the sea.

The Micmac moved around during the year, following the seasons and the animals. In spring, they fished the rivers for spawning smelt, trout, salmon, and sturgeon. In summer, they moved to the ocean, gathering birds' eggs and young fledglings from the rocky cliffs and feasting on fish, shellfish, and lobster. In fall, they speared eels wriggling down rivers to the ocean. In winter, they took to the woods which sheltered them from the freezing Atlantic winds. There, they hunted moose, caribou, otter, bear, and beaver.

The seasons that the Micmac followed for each type of fish, bird, and mammal were very regular. In fact, they were so regular that the Micmac built them into their language to express time. The Micmac did not say, "It is July" or "It is September." They said, "It is the moon when seafowl shed their feathers" or "It is the moon of moose-calling." A Micmac could not even talk about the time of year without talking about the hunting and fishing seasons.

Look at the Micmac calendar. It shows the names that the Micmac gave to each month of the year.

In winter, the Micmac used snowshoes and toboggans to move around their country. In summer, they travelled in canoes. The canoes were especially made for use on the ocean. Their high sides kept the waves from washing in.

Micmac houses were called wigwams. They were made of poles bound together at the top to make a cone shape. Usually the pole frames were covered with sheets of birchbark, overlapped like shingles and sewn together with spruce roots. Sometimes in summer, the people used mats of reeds to cover their houses. The mats kept the houses cool. They were so tightly woven that no rain could pass through them.

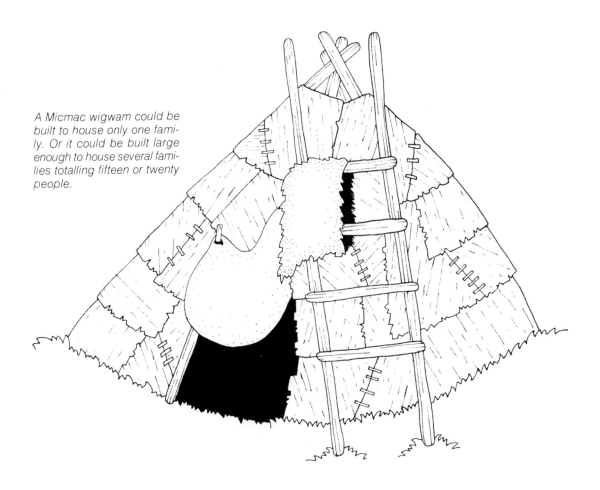

A Micmac wigwam could be built to house only one family. Or it could be built large enough to house several families totalling fifteen or twenty people.

MICMAC CALENDAR

January	frost-fish or spawn of tomcod
February	snow-blinding, sore eyes, or strong cold weather
March	springtime beginning
April	egg-laying, bird-hatching, or making maple sugar
May	young seals, frogs croaking, everything growing
June	leaf-opening
July	seafowl shed their feathers
August	young birds are full-fledged
September	moose-calling
October	fat, tame animals
November	tomcod moon
December	the chief moon

Indeed, the Micmac were skilled weavers. They wove many baskets — all shapes and sizes — from rushes and spruce root. They also made baskets out of birchbark. They folded the bark like a wallet and sewed it together at the edges.

The reason the Micmac made so many baskets was to store preserved foods. They had to store foods, for game was sometimes scarce in winter. Then, it was a good idea to have laid aside extra food from the summer surplus.

Micmac bark baskets. Designs were made on birchbark baskets by cutting away some of the top layer of bark so that the darker underbark was exposed.

The Micmac kept storehouses throughout their land. They left their extra food there rather than carry it with them. The storehouses were filled to the brim with preserved foods. Boxes of smoked fish and seal fat were piled on the floor. Sacks of dried, smoked moosemeat, some mixed with berries, hung from the ceiling. In between were racks of smoked eels dangling from sticks, the points thrust through their lower jaws. They looked like rows of sausages hanging in a meat shop.

The Micmac respected each other's storehouses. They never took anything that did not belong to them unless they were starving.

For most of the year, the Micmac travelled in small groups. Each group was led by a chief. But in summer, the groups came together for their annual festival.

Everyone looked forward to the summer festival. It was a time for feasting and celebration, for making new friends and keeping up with old ones. Children listened to stories about the past and legends of the Micmac hero, Glooscap, and his adventures with the animals. The grown-ups liked to tell stories about their family ancestors. Some of their stories had been handed down to them over twenty generations.

At the end of the summer festival, everyone had a better idea of what it meant to be a Micmac. The stories and the talk linked together the scattered people.

Summer was also a time for making marriages between the groups. Marriage was a serious business in Micmac society. It was considered an important way of linking the people. Therefore, the whole nation took an interest in it.

Most of the time, boys and girls were kept apart. Girls always came into a wigwam through a different door than boys. Boys seldom spoke to girls. Conversation was permitted only between engaged or married couples.

How then were a young man and woman to get together? This was the job of the chief's assistant, the "Watcher of the Young People." At the summer festival, he kept an eye open for young people. When he spotted a young man and woman smiling at each other, or showing other signs of interest, he told the chief and arranged an introduction. Then, the chief brought the couple and their families into his wigwam. He gave them advice on how to live together peacefully without quarrelling.

Because marriage was so important to Micmac society, everyone wanted to be sure that a couple was well-matched. So, for a year, the young man went to live with the girl's family. It was a hard year for him. He had to be on his best behavior. He had to show that he was a good hunter and could provide for a family. The father wanted to make sure that his daughter and the young man could get along with each other. At the end of the year, if the match looked good, the couple was married. But even at the last minute, at the wedding feast, both the young man and woman could change their minds. And divorce was allowed if the couple were unhappy later.

In Micmac society, men and women regarded each other as equals. They often hunted and fished together. But equal did not mean the same. Women had their own ways and customs which were different from men's. This is one Micmac man's view of women's ways.

> The women are great people for water. They fill barrels and buckets and rainspouts with it whenever they can get it. If it rained a year and there was water everywhere, I believe the women would be out "picking" water all the time. They are different from us, and they understand their own way. But we men don't understand the women's way.

(W.D. Wallis and R.S. Wallis, The Micmac Indians of Eastern Canada [Minneapolis: University of Minnesota Press, 1955])

According to legend, women were the inventors in Micmac society. They were credited with inventing the eel spear and with discovering how to make fire, how to make snowshoes, how to weave, and how to plant corn.

Women also spoke the most beautiful form of the language. The Micmac loved to play with language. They loved to make up words that were expressive and rich in images. Their language made it possible for them to constantly make up new words. There were many prefixes and suffixes that could be arranged in new and interesting combinations. To describe the way a person looked, for example, there were Micmac words that meant "a large-nosed person," a long-tongued person," and "a person who walks with toes turned out."

When the French came, they complained about this. They didn't like the Micmac habit of observing physical features and making up new names for them. Father Biard, a French priest, said:

> Any of our people who have some defect, such as the one-eyed, squint-eyed, and flat-nosed, are immediately noticed by them and greatly derided, especially behind our backs . . . [they] have a word and a nickname very readily at command.

(H.F. McGee, The Native Peoples of Atlantic Canada [Toronto: McClelland and Stewart, 1974])

The Micmac Meet Europeans

One night, a young Micmac woman had a dream. She dreamt that she saw a small island floating in to land. The island was covered with tall trees. Strange creatures were climbing in the trees. They looked like bears.

When she awoke the next morning, she told others about her dream. And to everyone's astonishment, there was the island drifting in towards the beach, just as the woman had described it. The men seized their weapons and sprang into their canoes. When they had paddled close to the island, they discovered that the bears were men.

The ship — for that was what the "island" really was — belonged to Jacques Cartier. He had been chosen by the King of France to explore the new land. The year was 1534.

The Micmac woman's dream. The Micmac believed that dreams foretold the future.

Cartier sailed along the Atlantic coast and around the Gaspé Peninsula. He went back to France with news of the abundant fish and minerals to be found in the new world. The next year, he returned and sailed up the St. Lawrence River as far as the Indian villages of Hochelaga and Stadacona, on the sites of what are now Montreal and Quebec City. In 1541, he made a third voyage, and tried to start a settlement near Stadacona.

The settlement failed. For the next sixty years, the French used the new land mainly as a fishing base. The Indians and the French fishermen only met each other when the fishermen came ashore to dry their catch and stretch their legs. The Indians didn't mind trading with these visitors who only dropped by for a short time, then sailed away.

Then, in the early 1600s, the French government decided to start a colony on the Atlantic coast, in the land they called Acadia. In 1604, colonists landed on Ste. Croix Island, just off the coast of what is now called New Brunswick. They spent a miserable winter. Thirty-five men died of scurvy. The next spring, they moved to the mainland (Nova Scotia). There, they founded the town of Port Royal.

The French in Port Royal suffered many hardships in the early years. Sometimes, only the Indians' help kept the settlers alive. The Micmac taught them how to hunt, and how to make snowshoes and birchbark canoes. They gave the settlers food when they had none and were hungry.

After a time, the French began trying to convert the Indians to Christianity. The French king had insisted on this when he gave permission to start the settlement. But the Micmac had doubts about the new religion. When they looked at the French sailors, many of whom were rough and unruly, they wondered whether Christianity would be good for them. And besides, they had their own religion.

However in 1611, Father Biard, a Jesuit priest, managed to win over Membertou, the head chief of all the Micmac living around Port Royal.

Membertou's son had fallen ill. His family had given him up for dead. They were holding a feast in his room to say goodbye when Father Biard came and persuaded them to give the patient to him. Then, in Father Biard's words, "a genuine miracle" occurred. "We put on the sufferer a bone taken from the precious relics of the glorified St. Lawrence . . . at the same time offering our vows for him, and then he improved." This convinced Membertou. He decided that there was power in Christianity. So he agreed to be baptized with his wife and children. They were the first Christian Indians in Canada.

Conversion to Christianity was just the first step. The priests also wanted to teach the Indians all about the new religion. This proved difficult because of the difference in languages. Even the most skilful interpreters had trouble translating European ideas into the Micmac language. The Micmac had many words for things a person could see or touch. But their way of expressing things a person could not see or touch was different. For example, they had their own way of expressing abstract ideas like wisdom, justice, mercy, and piety.

The French priests could not understand this. They decided that, since they did not have certain kinds of words, the Micmac were simple-minded.

The Micmac solved the language problem by adopting French words into their own language. For example, they had no word for goodbye. If a person was leaving, that was obvious. There was no need to say anything about it. But the French thought saying goodbye was important, so the Micmac adopted the French word for leave taking, adieu. In Micmac, it became *Adu* and *adeawiktak*, "to say goodbye."

In 1613, the French went to war with the British. Each side wanted exclusive control of the rich fishing grounds, lumber industry, and fur trade. The war went on for many years. During that time, Acadia changed hands several times.

The Micmac helped the French in their war with the British. They did not like the way the British established settlements farther south in New England by pushing the Indians off the land. They preferred the French who came mainly to trade and fish.

The term "Wabnaki" originally referred to a group of Indians living in what is now the American state of Maine. Over time, it referred to the loosely allied nations of the Atlantic region of which the Micmac were one.

The Micmac joined other Indians in Acadia and New England to form the Wabnaki Confederacy. When the British raided Acadia or tried to set up trading posts, the Confederacy fought back. The British then brought in their own Indian allies, the Iroquois. This led to battles between the two groups of Indians.

The war went on from time to time for 150 years. Finally, in 1759, the French were defeated at Quebec. And in 1763, a peace treaty was signed. Most of France's land in northern North America became the property of the British.

The Micmac signed a peace treaty with the British, too. They had been weakened by years of fighting. Many warriors had died in battles. Disease had also taken many lives. In 1746, for example, a typhus epidemic killed one-third of all the Micmac. So, once the French had been defeated, the Micmac had little choice but to make peace with the British.

The islands of St. Pierre and Miquelon off the south coast of Newfoundland remained French, and are still French today.

British settlers soon moved into the area and claimed the

22

land as their own. The Indians appealed for and were granted, little by little, some small reserves.

Despite British settlement, the Micmac refused to change their customs. They continued to live in their wigwams, to hunt, to fish, and to speak their language. They also resisted British attempts to teach them how to farm. Instead, they developed a business in what they were good at — making baskets and woodenware. They made barrels, buckets, and mast hoops to supply the magnificent sailing ships built on the Atlantic coast. The women made ash-splint baskets for potatoes and apples. These were eagerly snatched up by the surrounding farmers.

Reserves are sections of land set aside for Indians to live on and use.

This Micmac woman is making an ash-splint basket. The two close-up drawings show her weaving thin strips of ash wood.

This Micmac man is displaying his potato-digging tools. Every year, the Micmac travel to Maine to harvest potatoes for American farmers.

The men also found work in the lumber industry. In the 1930s, however, the shipbuilding and lumber industries collapsed. As a result, the Micmac started travelling to Maine every spring to harvest potatoes, returning to their reserves in the fall. They still do this today.

There are about 12 000 Micmac in Canada now. Many live on reserves in New Brunswick, Nova Scotia, Prince Edward Island, and Quebec. There is also a small settlement of Micmac in Newfoundland, although they have no reserve.

Fishing and farming employ many Micmac today. The women still gather in the band halls to make baskets of all shapes and sizes. Some are woven from strips of ash trees. Others are made of birchbark. These baskets are sold all over Canada. Some of the finest ones are displayed in museums.

All Native population figures in this book are estimates based on a study done by the Department of Indian Affairs. The study projects an eighteen percent increase in numbers of people between 1978 and 1990.

3 The Huron of the Great Lakes Region

Throughout eastern Canada, most Indians spoke Algonkian languages. They lived by hunting, fishing, and gathering wild plants. And they moved around all the time.

But one group of people was different. They spoke Iroquoian languages and were farmers. They seldom moved around and lived mainly by growing vegetables, especially corn. About three-quarters of their food came from their crops.

The farmers lived in what is now called southern Ontario, and along the St. Lawrence River. The land here is mostly covered by hardwood trees such as maple, oak, and birch. It is called the *Great Lakes* region.

There were four nations of farmers in the Great Lakes region: the Wendat ("Dwellers on the Peninsula") who the French called the Huron; the Tionontati or Tobacco Huron; the Attiwandaron or Neutral Indians; and the Iroquois. In this chapter, we will study one of these nations, the Huron, to see what their life was like.

*　　　*　　　*

Why were the Huron farmers rather than hunters?

One reason is the good climate. Temperatures in the region are mild, and rainfall is plentiful. The growing season — the time between winter frosts — lasts about 200 days. This is long enough to ensure a successful harvest in most years.

Another reason is that the soil of the Great Lakes region is just right for growing crops. The Huron lived south of Georgian Bay near Lake Simcoe. The land in this area is sandy and well drained. It is not as fertile as the land farther south, but it is easy to dig. This made working the fields easier for the Huron. They were less likely to break their tools which were mainly made of wood, bone, and shell.

Still another reason why the Huron became farmers was that they had seeds. You might think that seeds were easy to

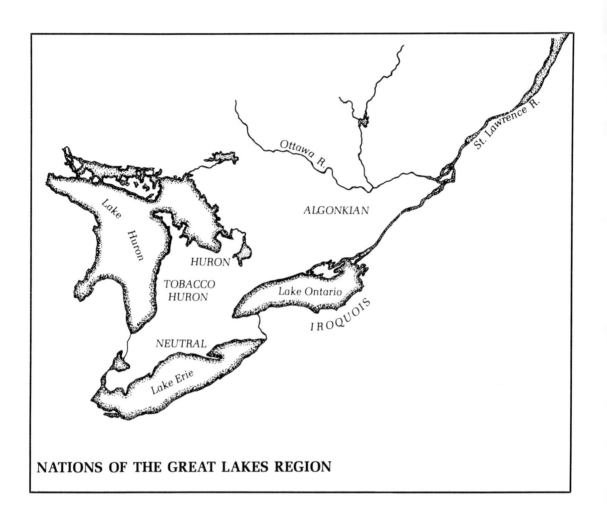

NATIONS OF THE GREAT LAKES REGION

get, but they weren't. The vegetables the Huron grew — corn, beans, and squash — did not originally come from Ontario. They came from what is now known as the southern United States and Mexico. There, these vegetables had grown wild. But the Indians in the south had learned how to "tame" these plants. They bred them to produce bigger and better vegetables than the wild kind. As time went by, the seeds and the knowledge of how to grow them were passed northward. Eventually, they reached the Huron living in southern Ontario. It took thousands of years for this to happen. Corn, beans, and squash were first developed in Mexico between 5000 and 2000 B.C. Corn did not reach southern Ontario until 1000 A.D. Beans and squash arrived about 1400 A.D.

The Huron and their Iroquoian neighbors were the first

Indians in Canada to live mainly by growing crops. Other nations in Canada at the time might have become farmers, too. They only needed the right soil and climate, and the knowledge of how to produce plants that could survive a short growing season.

Becoming farmers brought changes to Huron life. For example, farming meant that they could live in a smaller area than hunters. When people live by hunting, they have to spread out across much territory to find enough game to eat. But when they farm, they can grow all the food they need in a smaller area.

Huronia, the Huron's homeland, was quite small. It stretched only fifty-six kilometres from east to west and thirty-two kilometres from north to south. Between twenty and thirty thousand people lived in this small area.

The Huron worked hard in their fields, and everyone shared the labor. Men cleared the land. Women planted the seeds and tended and harvested the crops. Children helped by chasing hungry birds and animals away from the fields.

The Huron had to clear new fields from time to time when the soil lost its richness. So the men were always busy clearing land. They began by cutting down small trees and undergrowth with stone axes. Larger trees were killed by cutting rings around the trunks and building fires at the roots. Seeds were often planted around the tree stumps.

There were many hectares of fields around Huron villages. Once, a French missionary got lost in a huge corn field while trying to find his way to the next village!

In the spring, women prepared for planting. First, they carefully cleared the fields of weeds and debris. Then, they started corn seeds growing by soaking them for several days. After the seeds had sprouted, they were planted in small mounds of earth with nine or ten kernels in each.

Squash was planted differently because it was easily killed by a late spring frost. To avoid this danger, the seeds were started in bark trays filled with powdered wood. The women kept the trays near the fire in their homes. When the weather was warm enough, the seedlings were transplanted to the fields.

Women and girls weeded the crops carefully during the summer. Fall, of course, was harvesting time. Ears of corn were picked and hung to dry. Once dry, the kernels were shelled from the cobs. Squash was cut into slices and kept in bins. Beans were stored along with dried fish and animal fat. The Huron had enough food to last for the winter and a surplus to trade with other Indian groups.

Other Indian nations in Canada were beginning to farm. For example, the Ojibwa who lived near the Huron planted some corn, but they did not tend it and they picked it green. Probably, the northward spread of farming was interrupted by the coming of the Europeans.

The Huron prepared many different dishes. The women had almost forty recipes for corn alone. Corn breads and pudding were favorites. Sometimes, the women added deer fat or fish to give a little more flavor. The Huron also gathered wild foods to add to their diet. Plums, berries, and different kinds of nuts were plentiful. Sometimes, the berries were dried and baked in small tasty cakes.

Huron women used a heavy piece of wood and a hollowed out section of a tree trunk to pound corn into flour. The flour was made into bread and other foods.

RECIPE FOR HURON CORN BREAD

Ingredients:

1 L of fresh whole corn kernels
250 mL of cooked kidney beans

Directions:

Boil the corn in water for half an hour. Take off the stove and drain. Put aside for a few hours until the kernels dry out. Convert the kernels into flour using a blender. Next shake the flour through a sifter to remove any large pieces. Then mix in the kidney beans. Pour in enough boiling water to make a stiff dough. Shape it into rough patties about 2-3 cm thick. Cook in boiling water for one hour.

This bread is very tasty eaten with butter and salt or jam. It keeps for about a week in the refrigerator. To reheat, just put in boiling water or fry in butter.

Perhaps because they ate mostly vegetables, the Huron eventually lost their taste for meat. When they did hunt, they were more interested in getting skins for clothing and fat for flavoring.

Sometimes they caught deer. This was done by driving them into a river or a large pen. The hunters often took only the skin and fat and left the meat. At other times, they killed bear and trapped beaver for their fur pelts.

Even so, the Huron could not find enough animals to make all their clothes. There were too many people living in a small area. For the rest of their clothing, they traded with their neighbors.

Everyone looked forward to meeting other nations and seeing what they had to trade. From the Algonkians in the north, the Huron could get winter clothes. These were often decorated with colored porcupine quills. The Neutral Indians in the southwest had black squirrel skins. These were perfect for making winter robes. In return, the Huron traded pottery and surplus vegetables.

Trading routes spread out in many directions from Huronia. When Europeans arrived, the Huron quickly became involved in the beaver trade.

Notice the line and dot designs on these clay pots. The Huron used small sticks to make the designs on their pots before the clay was baked hard by fire.

There were several large villages in Huronia. Each had as many as 2000 people. There were also many smaller villages. Huron homes were long, high buildings. Because of their shape, they were called "longhouses."

Longhouses were very smoky inside. Up to ten families lived in a longhouse and each family had its own fire. In fact, fire was the biggest problem in these villages made of wood. Sometimes whole villages burned down. The Huron did their best to prevent this. They built their houses in the direction of the prevailing winds. That way, the sparks from the fires would not blow from one house to another. But just to be sure, they kept all their valuable possessions buried. In this way, they would not burn if their longhouse went up in flames.

When many people live close together, problems can arise. They need rules to help them get along with each other. There have to be leaders to make decisions.

In the case of the Huron, their society was divided into eight groups of related people. These groups were called "clans." Everyone belonged to one of these clans. The chief of each clan sat on a council of older men that governed each village. The village council met often, perhaps even every day. They arranged feasts and dances, judged disputes between the people, made sure no families went hungry, and planned buildings.

Sometimes the entire Huron nation held a meeting. Such meetings were very formal but friendly.

The subject of the meeting was always announced beforehand. Then, the men of each village consulted one another to decide who their spokesman would be and what he should say. A meeting began with a welcome to the chiefs from other villages. The hosts offered thanks because the visitors had arrived safely without being attacked by enemies or falling into a stream. Meetings often went on far into the night. Discussion continued until everyone was pleased.

When the French came to Huronia, they were puzzled and amazed by the Huron's orderly way of life. They found it hard to believe that thousands of people could live together without prisons, punishment, or even police! All of these were needed to keep the peace in France.

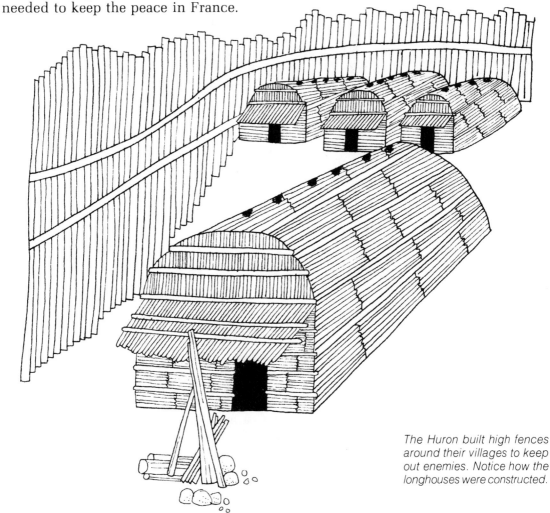

The Huron built high fences around their villages to keep out enemies. Notice how the longhouses were constructed.

The Huron Meet Europeans

The Huron came into contact with Europeans long before many other Indians in Canada. Their main contact was with the French, who settled along the St. Lawrence River.

French explorers travelled through Huronia many times. However, the Huron's main contact was with two groups: French missionaries and fur traders. These two groups were to have an important effect on the future of the Huron nation.

The first missionary in Huronia was a Récollet priest. His name was Joseph Le Caron. Father Le Caron arrived in 1615 and stayed with the Huron for a year before leaving. Sometime later, he returned to Huronia with two other Récollets to found a mission. Soon after, the Récollets at Huronia were joined by several Jesuit priests. The missionaries felt it was their duty to convert the Indians to Christianity. So they worked to turn the Huron away from their own religion.

The Huron believed in a god they called Yoscaha. Yoscaha lived in the sky. He had created the world and the Huron people. They also believed in spirits called oki, who might be good or evil. The spirits appeared to human beings in dreams, the language of the soul. The Huron believed that dreams foretold the future and gave advice on how to behave. After death, people's souls went to villages in the sky. Their campfires could be seen in the sky at night. There, in that heavenly world, life went on much as it had on earth. However, the Huron felt that the souls of the dead could not leave on this journey without a ceremony. It was called "the Feast of the Dead." During the ceremony, the bodies of the dead were taken out of their individual graves and buried in a common grave. With them were buried all the things they would need for a happy afterlife.

It is difficult to know how much success the missionaries had in converting the Huron. Certainly some became Christians. But, for a long time, the Huron held fast to their own religion. Only after their old way of life was destroyed by enemies did large numbers of Huron convert to Christianity.

The fur traders were the second group of French who contacted the Huron. These men were interested in making money from beaver pelts. The pelts were shipped to France, sold there, and used to make expensive beaver hats, which were in fashion at the time.

The Huron did not have many beaver in their own country. So they traded with the Algonkians to the north who had beaver and other furs. The Huron became go-betweens. They got furs from northern peoples and traded them with the French.

A Récollet was a member of a Catholic religious order formed in France about 1540.

A Jesuit was a member of a Catholic religious order founded in 1534. Jesuits often accompanied explorers and settlers to a new land. They were famous for their work as missionaries and leaders.

French priests came to live with the Huron. The priests felt it was their duty to convert the Indians to Christianity.

The fur trade made the Huron wealthy. It earned them many things that made their lives easier. From the French, they got iron hoes. These replaced their fragile tools of bone and shell. They also got iron knives, axes, and arrowheads to replace their brittle stone ones. The brass kettles of the French lasted longer than the Huron's clay pots. The women liked to wear the brass rings and bracelets and the brightly-colored porcelain beads that the French made. The Huron even acquired such new foods as peas and watermelons. And such animals as cats, pigs, geese, and chickens.

The Huron, however, did not enjoy their new wealth for very long. Along with trade goods, the French brought diseases that were new to North America. As a result, many Huron died in epidemics of smallpox and measles.

Even more serious was war. The fur trade caused many battles that finally broke up the Huron nation. To understand why, we must look at the relationship between Indians and Europeans at the time.

Two European nations, the British and the French, were struggling for ownership of North America. Both wanted control of the entire fur trade. And both drew their Indian allies into the struggle.

The French lived along the St. Lawrence River. Their allies were the Huron. The British had settled in what is now the United States. Their allies were the Iroquois, who lived south of Lakes Erie and Ontario.

The Iroquois were very like the Huron in their way of life. They spoke Iroquoian languages and were also farmers and traders. Historically, the two groups had always feuded with each other. The feud became worse as the fur trade with the Europeans increased. Beaver became scarce in Iroquois' lands. So the Iroquois were determined to take over the rich, northern fur supply that was controlled by the Huron.

The Iroquois made a series of attacks on the Huron. In time, they won the fur-trade war. This was mainly because they were able to get more guns from the British. The British were very pleased that the war was hurting their own enemies, the French.

By 1649, the Huron were forced to leave their villages and fields. Many died from lack of food. A few found refuge with neighboring nations. Some even went to live with their former enemies. They became adopted members of the Iroquois nation. One group fled with their missionaries to Ile Sainte Marie in Georgian Bay. They stayed there for one difficult winter. Then, they moved to Quebec City where the French could protect them. Yet another group travelled far. They finally ended up in what is now the American state of Oklahoma.

It took only forty years of contact with Europeans to bring an end to the traditional lifestyle of the Huron. Someday, you may read about the six Jesuit martyrs who died with the Huron. When you do, think about the thousands of Huron who lost their lives or their homes. Who in fact were the martyrs? The meaning of history can be different, depending on the point of view.

If the Huron nation was broken up more than 300 years ago, how do we know so much about it?

One source of information is the writings of explorers and missionaries. Every year the Jesuit missionaries sent their superiors in France long reports. They were called *Relations*. In French, "relations" means "report". The *Relations* described what life was like in the Huron villages, how the Huron thought, and what they believed.

Today, these writings are the basis for much of our knowledge about the Huron. However, they must be read with care. In Jesuit eyes, the Indians were "heathens" with strange, wild customs. This view influenced what they wrote. So when we read the Jesuit *Relations*, we must try to separate the facts from the biases.

We also learn about the Huron from archaeology. By digging up their villages, we can find out how they built their homes. We can also find out what kinds of things they made and what kinds of food they ate. Often, the missionaries did not bother to mention these things in their reports.

In Ontario, a Huron village has been rebuilt. It is called "Sainte-Marie among the Hurons." Missionaries started the original village in 1639. Someday, you might visit it to see for yourself how the Huron lived.

Another way we learn about the Huron is by talking to their descendants. There are Huron people living at Lorette, near Quebec City, who remember some of the old ways.

Now, there are almost 2000 Huron at Lorette. Their reserve lies just north of Quebec City. It is too small to farm, so they run such businesses as making canoes, snowshoes, and moccasins. These are sold across Canada and also in other parts of the world.

A martyr is one who suffers death for the sake of belief in a creed or religion.

The archaeologists must be careful not to damage the things they find, and they must follow rules on how to do their work.

4 The Ojibwa of the Northern Forest Region

One of the largest regions in Canada is the *northern forest*. It is a belt of forest land stretching from Labrador to the Yukon Territory, and from the prairies and the Great Lakes to the northern tree line.

The northern forest is a beautiful land. It is dotted and cut with thousands of lakes and rivers. Many kinds of animals make their homes here. There are moose, bear, beaver, caribou, mink, otter, wolverine, muskrat, porcupine, rabbits, deer, wolf, fox, and marten.

Many nations lived in the northern forest. They are divided into two main groups, according to language family. The speakers of Algonkian languages lived across Canada from Labrador in the east to Alberta in the west. They were the Montagnais, Naskapi, Abenakis, Ottawa, Algonkin, Ojibwa, and Cree.

The speakers of Athapaskan languages lived north and west of the Algonkian group. They were the Sekani, Chipewyan, Yellowknife, Slavey, Dogrib, Hare, Nahani, Beaver, Loucheux, Tutchone, Han, and Kaska.

One of the largest nations of the northern forest was the Ojibwa. In this chapter, we will study how the Ojibwa lived.

*　　　*　　　*

According to their legends, the Ojibwa originally came from the eastern seacoast. They migrated westward up the St. Lawrence river and the Great Lakes. For many years, they lived in the area around Lake Superior and north of Lake Huron. After 1649, when the Huron nation had been scattered, they also moved into the land that is now called southern Ontario.

The name *Ojibwa* may mean "people whose mocassins have puckered seams." It was probably given to them by other Indians, when they saw the marks that the seams of Ojibwa

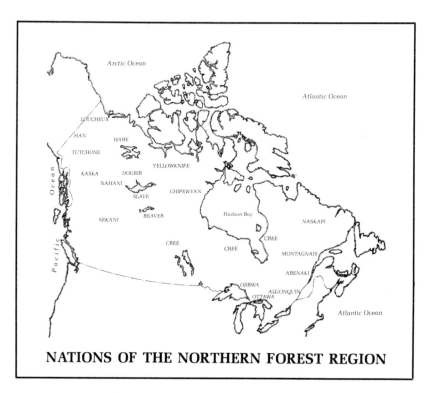

NATIONS OF THE NORTHERN FOREST REGION

moccasins made in soft ground. The Ojibwa name for themselves was *Anicinabe*, meaning "original people."

The Ojibwa lived mainly by hunting and fishing. They had to kill many animals to survive. For one day's food, a band of fifty Ojibwa needed two deer, forty rabbits, or 100 kg of fish. If the band killed a bear, there was enough food for two days. An elk supplied four days' food, and a moose, five.

With so much food needed, the Ojibwa had to be very skilful hunters. They used bows and arrows, snares, and traps to catch animals. But there was more to hunting than being skilful with traps and weapons. The Ojibwa had to be wise in the ways of the woods. They had to know how the animals lived, what they liked to eat, and where they fed. The hunters had to learn what paths the animals travelled, and where they were likely to be at certain times of the year.

To be a clever hunter took years to learn. Ojibwa children learned the skills of hunting from their parents. A boy hunted with his father almost as soon as he could walk. Mothers taught their daughters how to snare animals and how to clean and dress the game for food. Then, in later years, grown children were able to provide for their own families and take care of their aging parents.

Ojibwa men sometimes wore pouches made of otter pelts.

In some places, fishing was as important as hunting. In the rapids at what is now called Sault Ste. Marie, Ontario, for example, there were enough fish to feed a band all year round. In other places, there were fewer fish. And they could only be caught at certain times of the year.

Sometimes the people fished with a bag-like net fastened at the end of a long pole. The fisherman stood in the bow of his canoe and, as it slid backwards over the rapids, scooped fish out of the water. Each scoop might bring as many as six or seven large fish. The canoe was soon filled to the brim.

In winter, the Ojibwa fished through holes they cut in the ice. Using carved wooden "minnows," they lured the fish to the holes. When the fish came near, they were speared. In spring, the Ojibwa enjoyed fish eggs. They considered these a special treat. Today, fish eggs are known around the world as caviar. They are considered a great delicacy.

Meat and fish weren't the only foods the Ojibwa ate. They also liked to eat different kinds of plants, especially corn and wild rice.

The Ojibwa may have learned to plant corn from the Huron. In spring, they cleared a patch of land and planted the seeds. They returned in fall to pick the corn. Often, because of the short northern growing season, there wasn't enough time for it to ripen. When this happened, they picked it green.

The Ojibwa also harvested wild rice. It is a kind of wild grass which grows in marshy land. Its grains, which are long, brown seeds, are cooked in the same way as ordinary rice.

The Ojibwa collected the wild rice in their canoes. They simply pulled the stalks of the plants over the edge and shook the grains into the canoe bottom. They also left some grains to fall into the water, to make sure of a crop for the next year. Some scientists think that the Ojibwa planted rice seeds throughout their land, wherever they found a marshy place where it was likely to grow.

Wild rice is a very popular food today. It is still grown and harvested mainly by Indians.

Maple sugar was another favorite food of the Ojibwa. They made it from the sap of the maple tree. Each family had its own stand of trees. In spring, they tapped the trees and collected the sap. The sap was then boiled down to make maple sugar. It was a popular food because it gave the Ojibwa something sweet to eat in the winter.

The Ojibwa found different types of food in different places and at different times. So they were constantly moving around their territory. In spring, they would find a good fishing river. When their fishing was done, they would move to their fields to plant corn. Next perhaps, they would collect wild berries. And in winter, it was off to the hunting grounds.

Because they needed to travel so much, the Ojibwa developed some ingenious aids to transportation. These were especially

Today, most Indians who harvest wild rice still do so from canoes. Although machines to harvest wild rice have been invented, they sometimes damage the rice.

A close-up of wild rice grains.

suited to the land and the climate. In summer, they used the birchbark canoe to travel the many lakes and rivers. So good was the design of the Ojibwa canoe that it is still used today. The main difference is that canvas, fibreglass, or metal are used in place of the fragile birchbark. In winter, the Ojibwa used snowshoes to travel over the frozen lakes and rivers. Snowshoes allowed them to walk easily on top of the snow rather than sink into it. And to carry their possessions, the Ojibwa used the toboggan.

Since they were on the move so much, the Ojibwa made their homes light and easy to carry. They called these homes

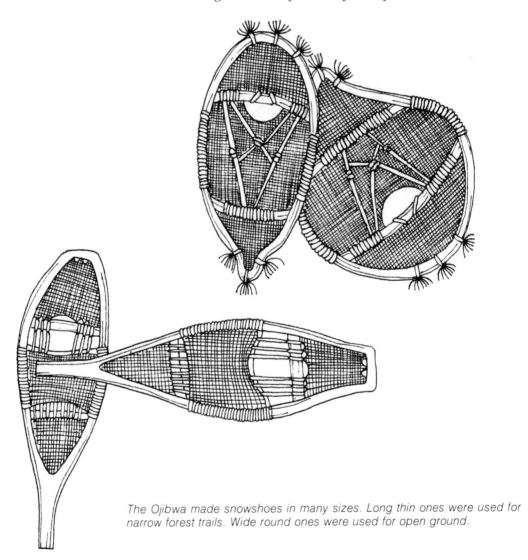

The Ojibwa made snowshoes in many sizes. Long thin ones were used for narrow forest trails. Wide round ones were used for open ground.

wigwams. They were made of bark or skins stretched over a frame of poles. When the Ojibwa moved, they usually left the tent poles in place. Wood was easy to find, so they could always cut new poles at their next campsite. Wigwams came in several shapes. Some were like domes, and others, like cones. Still others were wedge-shaped.

Most of the time, the Ojibwa travelled in small groups. In winter, they split up into family groups. A family group might include a mother and father, their children, and the father's parents. In spring, the families came together to form bands. Some bands were quite small, perhaps a few related families. Others were as large as several hundred people.

Although each band and family was quite independent, the Ojibwa had one organization which united them. It was called the *Midewewin* or *Grand Medicine Society.*

The Midewewin was a religious organization. It was devoted to healing the sick and teaching the right way to live. Its principal belief was that the proper use of herbs and living in harmony with nature would lead to a long life.

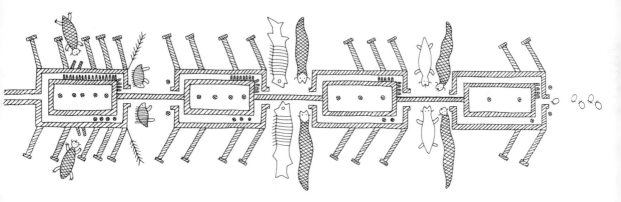

Members of the Society were taught moderate speech, quiet manners, and self-restraint. Lying, stealing and, later, the use of liquor, were strictly forbidden. Respect towards the Society and towards women was particularly stressed.

Membership in the Midewewin was open to both men and women. There were eight grades. Each grade required a long period of study and the payment of heavy fees. Only a few people ever reached the top grade.

The members, called *mede*, were the doctors of their communities. They knew many herbal remedies to cure disease. Also, they were skilled in ceremonies which related to the spirit world. Older people who were trained in the Midewewin were noted for their gentle voices, patience, and courtesy.

Midewewin scrolls like this one were often drawn on birchbark. This particular design shows the four houses (grades) of the Midewewin Society. Animals guard the doors of each house.

The Ojibwa Meet Europeans

The Ojibwa survived the coming of the Europeans better than most Indians in Canada. There are several reasons for this.

One reason is the land. The land in northern Ontario is not good for farming. Therefore, it did not interest European settlers. So, the Ojibwa living in this area were able to keep their land and their traditional lifestyle for a longer time.

In southern Ontario, however, the situation was different. There, the land is good for farming, and so settlers moved in. The Ojibwa living in this area had to adjust to a large migration of settlers within a very few years. By 1791, for example, there were 14 000 settlers, by 1812 there were 90 000, and by 1838, the population was 400 000 in this area.

Imagine how this must have looked through Ojibwa eyes. One year you were happily going about your business, looking after your family, and eating well. The next year, thousands of strangers move in. They cut down the trees that shade and shelter you, and kill off the animals you need for food. They have strange customs and bad habits, like drinking liquor. If you complain, they tell you that your way of doing things is no good, and that you should start living like them. There are too many of them for you to fight, and thousands more arriving every year. And besides, they have guns. What would you do? How would you adjust?

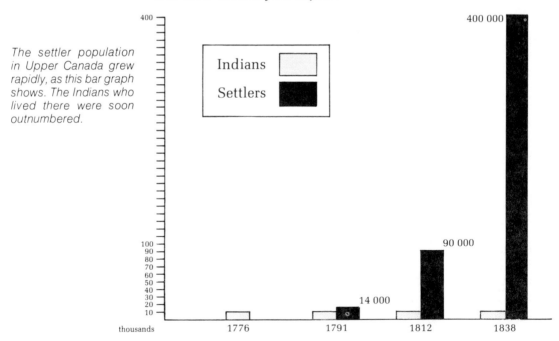

The settler population in Upper Canada grew rapidly, as this bar graph shows. The Indians who lived there were soon outnumbered.

The southern Ojibwa had help from their own people. They turned to the young men who had been educated by the Europeans and who understood European ways. Many young Ojibwa men joined the Methodist Church, one of the most politically active groups at the time. The Methodists taught them to become missionaries and teachers. They also supported them in battles with the Government.

The young men provided leadership when the Ojibwa were trying to get used to settlement. They fought for their people's rights with Government officials. They taught their people new ways of making a living, since the settlers had cleared the land, making hunting difficult. Without their leaders' help, it is likely that the Ojibwa would have suffered from European settlement much more than they did.

One of the most interesting of these men is Peter Jones. This is his story. It is taken from his diary, which tells what happened to his people, how he felt about the changes, and what he did to help his people adjust.

Peter Jones was born near Hamilton, Ontario in 1802. His father was Augustus Jones, who was Welsh. His mother was a Mississauga Ojibwa woman named Tuhbenahneequay.

Peter was raised by his mother. As a baby, he was initiated into his mother's clan, the Eagles. He was given the Ojibwa name Kahkewaquonaby, which means "sacred, waving feathers." As part of the ceremony, the little child was given some feathers "plucked from the eagle, the sacred bird."

As he grew older, Peter learned his people's ways. By the time he was six, he could handle a bow and arrow, throw a spear, and paddle a canoe. He was also taught how to use a gun. And most important, he learned "the nature of the various animals, the kind of ground they occupy, when they are likely to be found eating, and when asleep." Peter Jones loved to hunt. He later wrote, "As I grew older, I became very fond of the gun and was considered a great hunter."

Peter's father believed that the Indian ways were dying. He thought that his son should learn the ways of the Europeans. So when he was fourteen, Peter was enrolled in a school at Saltfleet, Ontario. At first, he could only understand a "few simple words" in English. But after nine months, he had learned to read and write. He then returned to his father's home on the Grand River to learn how to farm.

At this time, Peter dreamed of becoming a clerk in an Indian trading store. But this was not to be. When some Methodist missionaries held a camp-meeting near his father's farm, Peter decided to attend. As a result, he became one of the first Ojibwa to convert to Christianity.

The Credit Reserve was
on the Credit River
near Toronto. In 1847,
the Credit Indian band
moved to the "New
Credit" reserve, which
adjoins the Six Nations
reserve near Brantford,
Ontario.

Later, Peter became a missionary. He travelled far and wide,
preaching to many Indian nations. Between trips, he returned
to the Credit reserve where his mother's people lived.

The Credit Indians made Peter a chief. In return, he taught
them how to farm and make crafts and tools for sale. By 1833,
the Credit people had built a sawmill and bought a ship. They
named their ship "Credit Chief." In it, they sailed up and
down Lake Ontario, selling their lumber to settlers.

Peter Jones spent the rest of his life working for his people.
He made many trips to Toronto to discuss their rights with
Government officials. He even went to England to give lec-
tures about the Ojibwa and to meet Queen Victoria.

A letter Peter wrote from England shows how strange English society looked through his eyes.

> No nation, I think, can be more fond of novelties or new things
> than the English are: they will gaze and look upon a *foreigner*
> as if he had just dropped down from the moon; . . . When my
> Indian name (kahkewaquonaby) is announced to attend any
> public meeting, so great is their curiousity that the place is
> always sure to be filled; and would be the same if notice was
> given that a man with his toes in his mouth would address a
> congregation in such a place and on such a day,
> . . . The fashion in dress varies and changes so often that I am
> unable to describe it — I will only say that the ladies of fashion
> wear very curious bonnets, which look something like a farm-
> er's scoop shovel, and when they walk in the tiptoe style, they
> put me in mind of the little snipes that run along the shores of
> the lakes and rivers in Canada. They also wear sleeves as big
> as bushel bags, which make them appear as if they had three
> bodies with one head.

(Christian Guardian, February 22, 1832, p.201.)

Peter Jones translated part of the Bible and many hymns
into Ojibwa. This way, his people could read them, in their
own language. He also wrote a history of his people. He felt it
was important to record the traditions he had learned as a
boy. And he felt that Europeans should be informed about the
value of Ojibwa culture. He helped to set up schools in which
Ojibwa children were taught both in their own language and
in English. Some of the school teachers were young Ojibwa.

During this time, Peter continued to live with his people.
He never stopped teaching them about their rights and helping
them to adjust to the European way of life. When he died in
1856, many of his friends, both European and Indian, attended
his funeral.

Certainly Peter Jones and the other Ojibwa Christian leaders could not solve all the problems. Rightly or wrongly, they believed that the Indian way was dying and that the future lay in following European ways. They understood both European and Indian ways of life. And they were able to find ways of bringing the two together. Their efforts gave the Ojibwa a head start in adapting to European society.

Today, the Ojibwa are one of the largest groups of Indians in Canada. They number about 70 000 in population. Only the Cree, with about 100 000, are greater in number.

In the north, many Ojibwa still live by hunting, fishing, and trapping. In summer, many find work fighting the hundreds of forest fires that start every year. The southern Ojibwa often farm their lands.

Recently, some Ojibwa have started to paint. Their art is becoming famous around the world. Their paintings often express traditional Midewewin ideas about people and nature.

5 The Blackfoot of the Prairie Region

East of the Rocky Mountains lies the region called the *prairie*. It is a stretch of high, flat land and covers southern Alberta, Saskatchewan, and Manitoba.

The mountains and the inland position of the prairie region keep out rain and warm winds from the Pacific Ocean. This makes the climate dry and the temperatures extreme. Few trees grow on the prairie, but there is plenty of short, rich grass. Vast herds of shaggy, brown buffalo once grazed on the prairie grass. The people of the prairie lived by hunting these buffalo.

The prairie nations were the Blackfoot, Assiniboine or Stony, Plains Cree, Sarcee, Saulteaux or Plains Ojibwa, and Gros Ventre. In this chapter, we will study the life of the Blackfoot.

The name Manitoba, may have come from an Ojibwa word "manitou bau," meaning "strait of the spirit."

* * *

The Blackfoot tell a story of their origin.

In the beginning, Old Man and Old Woman decided to make people. Old Man was cranky. He insisted that he should have the first say in everything. Old Woman agreed as long as she could have the second say.

"Let the people have eyes and mouths in their faces," said Old Man, "and let their eyes and mouths run straight up and down."

"Yes, let them have eyes and mouths, but they should run from side to side in their faces," added Old Woman.

"Let the people have ten fingers on each hand," Old Man decided.

"No," declared Old Woman. "Ten fingers are too many. They will just be in the way. Let them have four fingers and a thumb on each hand."

And so the people were made. Imagine what they all would have looked like if Old Man had had his way!

51

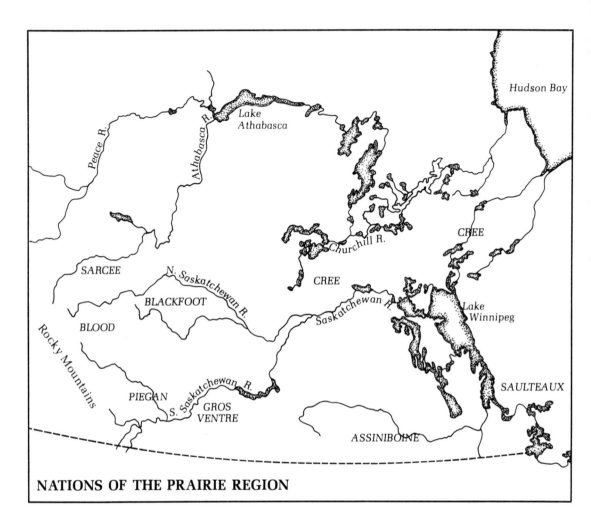

NATIONS OF THE PRAIRIE REGION

The Blackfoot didn't always live in the prairie region. They once lived in the timber country around Lesser Slave Lake. Long ago, they moved south and west until they reached the foot of the Rocky Mountains. This became their homeland.

The name "Blackfoot" came from the Indians' own name for themselves, *Siksika*. It means "dark moccasins." Blackfoot moccasins were probably either painted black or were covered with black dust left from prairie fires.

The Blackfoot nation was made up of three groups: the Blackfoot, the Blood, and the Piegan. The three groups were linked by a common Algonkian language, common customs, and by frequent intermarriage. Generally, each group went its own way. But when threatened by an enemy, they joined together to present a united front.

The main source of food of the Blackfoot was the buffalo. Since the buffalo moved around, the people had to travel all the time to follow them.

On the march, the men walked ahead. They carried only their weapons so they could be ready to hunt game at a moment's notice. The women walked behind carrying babies and heavy bundles of goods. Big dogs pulled the rest of their possessions on travois, made of tipi poles. A strong dog could pull as much as thirty-two kilograms. Sometimes, however, the dogs were a real nuisance. They liked to fight among each other and often went bounding off after other animals. Thus, the Blackfoot were forced to travel very slowly. Eight or nine kilometres was considered a good day's march. And since the women and the dogs could carry or pull only so much, the Blackfoot could not keep many possessions.

Horses pulled Blackfoot travois which were made of long poles tied together. The Blackfoot also used the poles to build tipis when they camped.

Another method of
hunting buffalo was
to chase them over
a cliff. They fell and
were killed.

When the men found a herd of buffalo, they went back to fetch the women. The women brought their dog travois and made a fence with the poles. After the men chased the buffalo into a corral, the women stood behind the fence shouting and waving their arms. The barking dogs and shouting women kept the buffalo from breaking through the fence, while the men rushed in to kill them with arrows and lances.

Driving the buffalo into a corral was not easy. Sometimes the big animals ran away in fear before the men could reach them. At other times, the buffalo were nowhere to be found. If they managed to kill many buffalo, the Blackfoot could live well through the long, cold winter. But if they killed too few, they might starve before spring.

The buffalo supplied almost all the needs of the Blackfoot people. Its rich dark meat was always a satisfying meal, and imaginative cooks loved to think up new recipes. It could be boiled or roasted over coals like a barbecue. It could be made into a kind of sausage or dried and spiced with berries and wild peppermint to make a food called pemmican for the winter.

The Blackfoot found many other uses for the buffalo. From the skin, the women made moccasins, braided ropes, tent covers, and clothing. Buffalo robes, with the hair still on, were used as blankets. The horns could be used as containers or carved into spoons and cups. The hair was braided into ropes or stuffed into saddles for padding. The sinews provided thread for sewing and strings for bows. Someone even discovered how to make yellow paint and dye from the buffalo's gall bladder.

While the Blackfoot preferred buffalo meat, they also hunted other animals. Deer, moose, elk, and smaller mammals were welcome when buffalo were scarce. Wild plants, especially roots in early summer and berries in the fall, varied their diet.

For many years, the Blackfoot lived on the edge of the prairie, slowly travelling around on foot in pursuit of buffalo. But when horses came to the plains, their way of living changed.

Horses had once lived in North America, but they had all died out during the ice ages. Then, in the 1500s, Spanish explorers brought horses with them to Mexico. Some of the horses escaped from the Spanish and were rounded up by Mexican Indians. The Mexican Indians, however, did not know how to use the horses. They thought they were a new kind of deer and killed them for food. Later on, the Spanish taught some Mexican Indians how to train and ride the horses. They also taught them how to make saddles and bridles. Gradually, the horses, along with the important knowledge of how

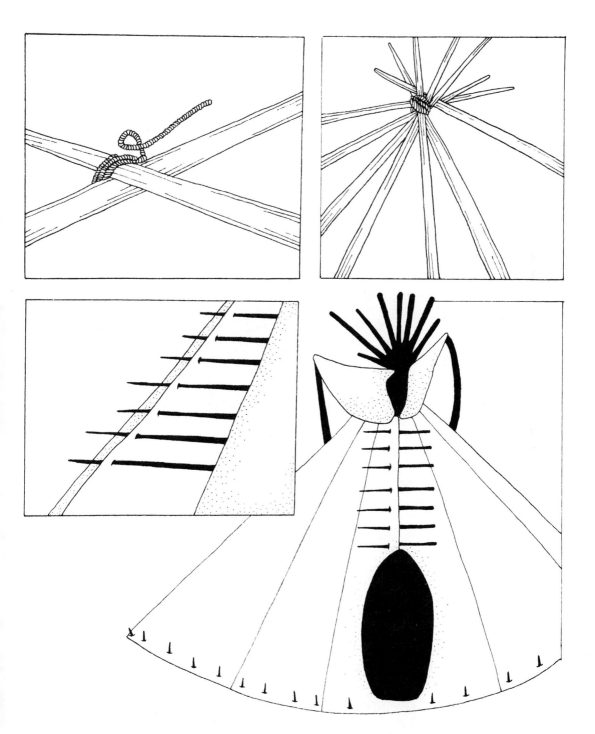

Blackfoot tipis were made of pole frames covered with buffalo hides. It took many hides to cover one tipi.

to use and care for them, spread north through the plains to other nations. This took almost 200 years. The Blackfoot began to use horses by about 1700.

Horses were ideally suited to the prairie. Like the buffalo, they lived by eating grass and could move freely across the wide open spaces. Indians who lived in wooded areas seldom used horses. There was little grass and few open spaces in the forests.

The horses reminded the Blackfoot of the dogs which carried their belongings. So, at first, they called them "big dogs." Later, they were renamed "elk dogs" because they were so much larger than dogs, and more useful.

Horses made life much easier for the Blackfoot. On horseback, they could travel fast and keep up with the buffalo herds. They no longer had to rely on corralling the buffalo to kill them, a method which often depended on luck. Instead, men on swift "buffalo-runners" could ride right into the middle of the herd and kill all the buffalo they needed.

Also, horses could pull or carry much heavier loads than dogs. So the Blackfoot were able to have more goods. They could have larger, more comfortable tipis, extra suits of decorated clothing, and more buffalo robes for winter. They could also carry extra food. Then, the people didn't have to worry about starvation.

Horses became so important to the Blackfoot that families started to measure their wealth by how many they owned. Most families owned about ten horses, since they needed that many to move camp. A wealthy man might have as many as fifty to one hundred horses. A poor family might have only one or two.

Poorer families looked to the wealthy to lend them extra horses. A wealthy man who was generous with his herd was admired by everyone. If he was also wise and brave, he might become a great chief. No one liked a wealthy man who was stingy.

The time came when the Blackfoot wanted more horses than they could breed in a short period of time. Sometimes, they satisfied their desire by trading with their neighbors. But, more often, they stole horses from their neighbors. In fact, raiding for horses became very important. An ambitious young man could show his bravery and skill by capturing many horses. If successful, he could start to build up a herd of his own. This would make him wealthy and respected. Unless a young man belonged to a family with many horses, raiding was the only way he could become rich.

Raids were usually organized by an experienced leader. He chose some trusted friends and together they set off for enemy territory. Once they found an enemy camp, the raiders waited until dark. Then, they stole in among the tipis. Everyone headed straight for the best horses — the buffalo-runners — which their owners kept tied up to their tipis. If there was time, the raiders also rounded up the ordinary horses. They were usually kept in a large herd nearby.

All this had to be done without waking the sleeping camp. It took courage, patience, and skill. Once they had quietly rounded up all the horses they wanted, the whole party set off for home. They rode as fast as they could, driving the captured horses before them.

The Blackfoot gained many horses by raiding. However, since their own horses were raided as well, they may have just come out even in the end.

Most Blackfoot warfare took place while raiding for horses. Once in a while, however, they fought pitched battles with other nations.

Before a battle began, the two sides lined up, facing each other. The men rode back and forth between the lines singing songs about how brave they were and hurling challenges and insults to their opponents. Then the two sides charged each other. Fighting went on until one side gave up.

Few people were killed in these battles. The warriors considered it a much greater honor to "count coup" on their opponents. "Coups" were considered acts of courage and skill and were ranked according to how daring they were. For example, everyone felt that a man with a gun was most dangerous. So capturing the gun without killing him was considered the highest honor. Taking away a bow, a shield, a war bonnet, a war shirt, or a pipe was also considered a high-ranking coup. Both sides valued these possessions and fought hard to keep them. Killing a man from a distance was considered a less valuable coup. It did not require as much bravery.

After the battle, the warriors feasted and described their coups. If there were witnesses to a particular warrior's daring, then he was granted the honor of counting coup. To receive this honor was a proud moment in a man's life.

At various times, the Blackfoot fought the Crow and Shoshone to the south, the Plains Cree and Assiniboine to the north and east, and the Kootenay and Salish to the west. Their only allies were the Sarcee and sometimes the Gros Ventre.

Why did the Blackfoot fight with their neighbors? Horses were probably the main cause. Before all these nations acquired horses, they lived on the edges of the prairie and seldom saw each other. But because the horse allowed them to follow the buffalo herds out onto the prairie, they came into closer contact. Soon, each nation claimed a large territory for its own. The claims led to conflict between the nations. The conflict was made even worse because every nation wanted to build up big horse herds. And the quickest way they could do this was by raiding each other.

Warfare and hunting had an effect on Blackfoot marriage. Because men were killed in battles or in hunting accidents, women outnumbered them. There were about three men for every five women. The Blackfoot found a sensible solution to this problem. A man who could provide enough food, shelter, and horses could marry several women. A poor man might have only one wife. Many men had two or three. And a wealthy man had as many as five wives. This system protected women whose husbands or sons were killed. The Blackfoot preferred to marry sisters. Sisters, they believed, were more likely to be happy together.

Raiding for horses also changed Blackfoot politics. Each Blackfoot band picked two chiefs — a peace chief and a war chief. The peace chief decided where the band would travel each day and settled arguments in camp. The war chief decided on matters of war. Before the Blackfoot acquired horses, there was little warfare. So they probably didn't need a war chief at that time.

The Blackfoot chiefs could not force their people to do anything. They held power only as long as the people agreed with their decisions and were willing to follow them. The people wanted their chief to be wise and generous to the poor. They also wanted him to be a holy man who could call on the spirits to help his nation.

Every young Blackfoot man hoped to find a spirit helper who would give him good advice, strength, and courage in times of trouble. At the age of about thirteen, a young Blackfoot went into the wilderness to seek a helper. There he stayed without food or water, praying to the powers of the sky, earth, and water to have pity on him. When he was exhausted and fell asleep, a spirit might appear in a dream. Usually, it took the form of an animal or a bird. Sometimes, it looked like a human being. The spirit promised to help the young man. It showed him the objects that were sacred to it. And it told him how to call on its power when in need. The young man bound the sacred objects together to form a "medicine bundle." He carried this with him for the rest of his life.

A Blackfoot warrior counted coup by touching his opponent with a long coup stick, like the one this warrior is holding.

The powers of the spirit helper were called on to bring success in hunting and in war. A great chief was one whose spirit helper was judged to be strong enough to lead the chief and his followers to victory.

Sometimes, young women fasted for a spirit helper, too. But usually it was young men. The Blackfoot believed that women had natural spiritual power, because they were the source of life. Men, they believed, had to make a special effort.

Blackfoot men began their search for a spirit helper when they were young. However, prayer and fasting went on throughout a man's entire life.

The Blackfoot Meet Europeans

The first European to meet the Blackfoot was an explorer from the Hudson's Bay Company. In 1754, the Company sent Anthony Henday, one of its employees, to persuade the Blackfoot to bring furs to Hudson Bay. The Blackfoot refused. They told Henday that they were quite happy hunting buffalo in their own country. Also, they were afraid of the long trip to Hudson Bay. They thought they might starve. And they would have to travel by canoes, which they didn't know how to use.

In 1772, the Company tried again. It sent the persuasive Mathew Cocking, another employee. Again, the Blackfoot refused. Finally, the Company decided that, if the Blackfoot would not come to it, it must go to the Blackfoot. So, in 1792, the Company built Buckingham House, the first trading post in the heart of Blackfoot territory.

The Company expected a rich harvest of beaver from the Blackfoot. There were many beaver in the streams of the prairie land. But the Blackfoot didn't want to hunt beaver. They considered it a sacred animal. However, they enjoyed hunting buffalo. So they offered buffalo meat, as well as horses, to the traders. In return, they wanted guns, ammunition, and tobacco.

The Hudson's Bay Company enforced its own version of law in the west. In 1869, however, it sold its vast territory to the Government of Canada. As a result, the land was without law for the next few years. During this time, American fur traders moved into Blackfoot country. They wanted buffalo skins to make robes and leather for the east. In return for the skins, the traders offered whisky to the Blackfoot.

The use of whisky led to many problems. For example, during the winter many Blackfoot froze to death when caught out on the open prairie while drunk. Many more traded away all their horses and their household goods for the whisky. Often, they were left with nothing to keep them alive in winter.

These were bad years for the Blackfoot. One observer estimated that one quarter of them died because of the whisky trade alone. Many more died from smallpox, which swept through the prairie people.

The situation was made worse by the fact that, within a few years, there were almost no buffalo left. Buffalo hunters, mostly in the United States, had killed many buffalo. As a result, the herds that once roamed the prairie grew small.

Without the great herds, the Blackfoot could no longer supply their basic needs.

The Canadian Government finally became aware of the lawless situation in the west. In 1873, it recruited men for the newly-formed Northwest Mounted Police. The police were sent into Blackfoot territory. When they arrived, most of the whisky traders closed their trading posts and ran. Others were arrested and sent to jail.

The Blackfoot chiefs were grateful to the Police for getting rid of the whisky traders. The chiefs agreed to work with the police. As Crowfoot, one of the leading chiefs, said:

> If the police had not come to this country, where would we be now? Bad men and whisky were killing us so fast that very few of us would have been left today. The police have protected us as the feathers of the bird protect it from the frosts of winter.

Crowfoot, the Blackfoot chief, was a famous orator. He led his people in treaty talks with Europeans. In his later years, he journeyed across Canada by train.

The Blackfoot and the Mounted Police needed this friendship and mutual respect. By 1877, settlers were moving west. In the United States, settlement had led to bloody conflicts with the Indians. The Canadian Government wanted to avoid such conflict in the West. So, it decided to make a treaty with the Blackfoot.

The treaty was called Treaty Number Seven. The Blackfoot agreed to give up the right to all their land. In return, they were granted reserves of 2.56 km² per family. They were also given money and cattle, seeds, and tools to begin farming. In making the treaty, the respect between the Blackfoot chiefs and the police played an important part.

The chiefs had a hard time persuading young Blackfoot men to settle down on reserves and become farmers. However, the elders believed that the old days had ended. The new way of life, they said, lay in living like the Europeans. They did not like it, but they felt they had no choice.

Since that time, many Blackfoot have become farmers and ranchers. They live on three big reserves in southern Alberta. Their numbers have increased considerably since the days of the fur trade. In 1809, there were only 5200 Blackfoot left. By 1978, there were almost 10 000.

The Blackfoot still keep herds of horses. Fast horses, once so important for chasing buffalo, are now used for herding cattle. They are also used for riding in rodeos, the Blackfoot's favorite summer sport.

6 The Haida of the Pacific Region

In the extreme west of Canada lies the *Pacific* region. Mountains and forests cover most of this region. Inland, there are deep, heavily wooded valleys. Long, narrow lakes and fast-flowing rivers cut through the mountains and the forests and empty into the Pacific Ocean. Off the rocky coast lie many islands, both large and small.

The climate of the Pacific region is mild. A current of warm water runs along the shore, warming the winds that blow across the land. Rainfall is heavy because the winds carry moisture from the ocean. The mountains block the winds and, with nowhere to go, rain falls on the coast.

The people of the Pacific region were fortunate. They lived in one of the richest areas in North America. The sea, the rivers, and the forests supplied more than their basic needs. So rich was the region that the people never had to travel far to find food. They could spend time doing other things, especially art, which they created in beautiful and complex forms.

Many groups of Indians lived in the Pacific region. Along the coast lived the Haida, Tsimshian, Tlingit, Kwakiutl, Nootka, Bella Coola, and Coast Salish. Inland, there were the Chilcotin, Carrier, Interior Salish, Tsetsaut, Kootenay, and Tahltan. In this chapter, we will study one group, the Haida, to see what their life was like.

*   *   *

The Haida lived in the northern part of the region on the Queen Charlotte Islands. Mountains rise sharply on the west side of the islands. Some are more than 1200 m high. These same mountains slope down to golden, sandy beaches in places on the east side.

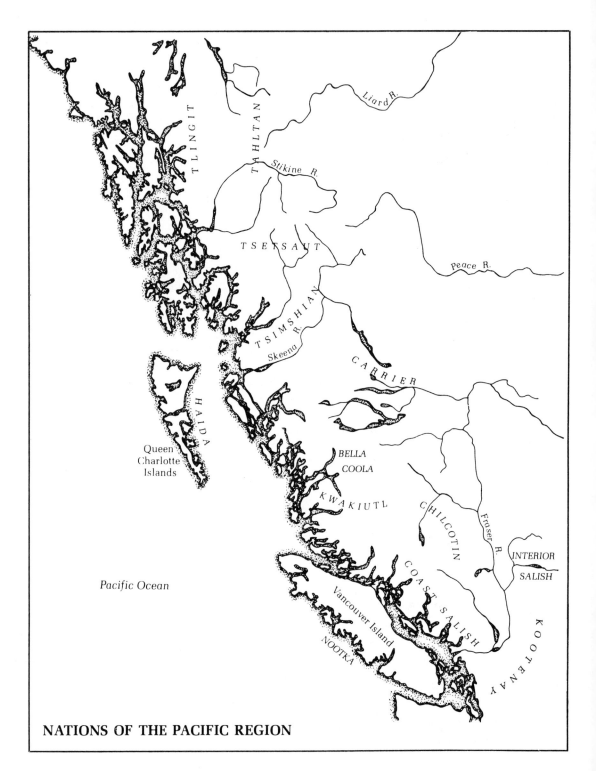

NATIONS OF THE PACIFIC REGION

The sea provided the Haida with more food than they could possibly use. Close to shore, they gathered such shellfish as clams and mussels and caught such fish as cod, halibut, and candlefish. The Haida caught salmon, too. In spring, the salmon swarmed up the rivers to breed. They came in such numbers that, as one explorer exclaimed, "You could walk across their backs." The Haida fished for the salmon in the streams and also caught them with hooks in the ocean. Farther out to sea, the Haida hunted such sea mammals as hair seals, sea lions, and sea otters.

The land supplied the Haida with many kinds of food, too. They gathered such things as nettle roots, berries, gull eggs, and a kind of edible clover.

With so many foods to eat, the Haida never had to worry about not having enough.

The warm, damp climate of the Pacific region encourages trees to grow. From the trees, especially the cedar, the Haida were able to supply almost all of their non-food needs.

Cedar was the perfect wood for these people, who had only stone or bone tools to work with. The wood, which is soft but very firm, is easy to work with. And the grain is so straight that the logs split evenly into planks. From cedar logs, the Haida made huge canoes which they used to travel up and down the coast. The canoes were up to eighteen metres long. And they could carry as much as two metric tonnes of cargo and as many as sixty passengers. From cedar planks, the Haida built houses that were twelve metres high and large enough for ten or more families to live in.

Cedar wood is full of natural oils. After the trees have been cut down, the oils preserve the wood. They make it very long-lasting, even in the damp climate of the Pacific coast. Some of the houses and totem poles built from cedar have lasted over a hundred years.

When steamed, cedar bends without breaking. The Haida made boxes and cooking pots from it. They moulded the wood to whatever shape they desired. They even made clothes from cedar bark, by weaving the fibres into blankets and robes.

The Haida lived in small villages on the shores of the islands. Usually, their villages consisted of several large houses. A number of related families lived together in each house.

Family relationships were very important to the Haida. Everyone belonged to one of two clans. They were either Eagles or Ravens. Children belonged to the same clan as their mothers. If a child's mother was a Raven, the child became a Raven too, even if the child's father was an Eagle.

Candlefish, also called oolichan, are small silvery fish rich in oil. The Haida, after drying them and pulling wicks through their bodies, burned them like candles. Hence, the name *candlefish*.

This system of tracing descent is called matrilineage.

*These Haida women are wearing cloaks made of shredded cedar bark.
Baskets also made of cedar bark are slung around their shoulders.*

When children grew up, they could marry only a person
from the other clan. Ravens had to marry Eagles and Eagles
had to marry Ravens. No one could marry a person from the
same clan. To want to do so would have been considered shocking, like marrying your own brother or sister. Later, when
Europeans came, a Christian missionary who did not understand this custom insisted on marrying two Eagles. The Haida
considered this a great scandal.

Each clan had its own traditions, symbols, and history. Members of a clan felt a great deal of pride in their clan backgrounds. And if they ever needed help, they knew they could call on their clan to support them. This social system gave each Haida a sense of security and belonging.

Within the clans, some people were more closely related than others. A group of closely related people were known as a "lineage." Usually, the people of one lineage lived together in one village.

Belonging to a lineage gave a Haida person many benefits. Each lineage owned the right to use certain hunting grounds, berry patches, and fishing places. A lineage also possessed ranks, titles, and important crests. Only members of a lineage had the right to display its crests on the front of their houses.

Some lineages were more important and of higher rank than others. From the highest lineages came the overall chiefs of the Haida. They inherited many of their titles from their mothers. These men had the right to special titles such as "village owner." From the lower lineages came the common people.

At the bottom of Haida society were the slaves. They were mostly people from other nations who had been captured in war. Haida slaves were usually treated well. Sometimes their families could buy them back. Other times, however, they were killed during important ceremonies. This, the Haida believed, proved a chief's wealth. It showed that he could afford to give up valuable property.

The Haida took rank very seriously. It was the basis of their government. They wanted to know where each person stood in relation to everyone else — who was of higher rank and who was of lower rank.

In a way, the Haida ranking system was set up like an arithmetic statement, like the following:

$$A > B > C > D. \ldots$$

No two people could be equal. Each person had his or her own place. However, sometimes it was difficult to decide exactly what each person's place was.

Even though people inherited the right to certain titles and ranks from their families, they had to prove that they were worthy of them. To do this, the Haida developed a custom called the "potlatch." A potlatch was a big gathering. The chief of one lineage invited the chief of another lineage and all his relatives. There was dancing and feasting. During the potlatch, the host gave huge amounts of food and valuable presents to all his guests. He hoped to achieve two goals by doing this. First, he wanted his guests to see the wealth, energy, and importance of both himself and his lineage. This would ensure that everyone would accept his right to a high title. Secondly, he wanted his guests to remember the event which the potlatch was given to celebrate. And the only way an event could be remembered was if it left a lasting impression in everyone's mind.

Potlatches were also held for other reasons. Sometimes they were held to celebrate the raising of a totem pole or the building of a new house. Sometimes they were held if something very shameful had happened to a member of a lineage. For example, if a person had been captured and made a slave by another nation. Then, a potlatch was held to wipe out the shame this brought on the other members of the lineage.

Potlaches were a great deal of work for the members of a lineage. Often the people worked for several years to gather all the presents. Sometimes, a lineage gave away almost everything it owned to make sure that its potlatch would be remembered. But the land was so rich that they were never poor for very long.

Another example of the Haida's use of cedar was the bentwood box. After steaming the cedar, it could be bent to make many different shapes and designs.

Can you recognize these abstract Haida carvings of a shark, a beaver, and a wolf?

Because there was so much food near at hand, the Haida didn't have to spend a lot of time hunting like other nations. Instead, they could spend time doing other things, like painting and carving. In fact, art became very important to the Haida. To be known as a great artist was one of the highest achievements a Haida could wish for.

The Haida felt that everything, even everyday items like spoons and bowls, should be decorated with carvings or paintings of spirits and animals. Sometimes, the decorations were done in a lifelike style. Anyone could see at a glance what animal the artist was thinking of. At other times, artists preferred to work in a more abstract style. This made it harder for a person to tell what a picture or carving represented. To help the observer, the artist provided clues. For example, a beaver painted or carved in an abstract style could always be recognized. Its scaly tail and large front teeth were always included in the design. An eagle was always shown with its curving beak. And a bear with its big paws with long, curving claws. All the Haida knew these clues. They could appreciate how the artist had taken the traditional designs and used them to create something new and different.

Besides smaller items like spoons and bowls, the Haida also decorated larger things like their houses and their canoes. However, their most famous artistic creations were totem poles.

Totem poles were made of logs of various length, some short and some very long. They were placed in front of the houses to display the family crests. Probably the Haida first made totem poles by painting crests on the front of the house, or by carving them into the poles and beams supporting the house. Later, they began carving and painting their designs on free-standing poles.

Totem poles have become the trademark of the people of the Pacific region. Many people think that all Indians made them. This is not true. Only in the Pacific region (and mainly along the coast) did Indians carve totem poles.

The Haida were particularly fond of totem poles. Charles Edenshaw, a great Haida carver, told this story about how the Haida learned to make them.

Many years ago, the Haida lived in cold and comfortless huts, without columns or any such things outside their dwellings. One day a chief, who seems to have been of more than ordinary intelligence, decided to make a more comfortable type of house.

While he was thinking over a plan, a spirit appeared to him. The spirit showed him a house with the measurements and every other detail complete except that there was no carved column (totem pole).

The chief and his tribe set to work and gathered the material they needed. Just as they were about to build, the spirit appeared to the chief again. The spirit showed him the same plan, but with the difference. In front of the house was a carved column. The chief's crest, a Raven, was carved on top. Underneath the Raven was a second carving, the crest of his wife, an Eagle. The spirit told the chief that all the people in every village were to build houses the same and to set up columns.

At first, only the wealthiest chiefs could afford totem poles. Using stone tools, it took a lot of time and labor to carve them. However, when Europeans came, they brought iron tools which made carving much easier. Soon, almost every Haida house had at least one totem pole. Some had two or three.

A Haida village with free-standing totem poles. Haida totem poles displayed family crests. Family lineages were also recorded on the poles. It is generally thought that totem poles, especially free-standing ones, became more common after the coming of Europeans. The Europeans supplied the Haida carvers with iron tools. These were much easier to work with than the traditional stone tools.

The Haida Meet Europeans

The first Europeans to come to the land of the Haida were Russians. They arrived between 1745 and 1762. The British and the Americans followed soon after.

The Europeans were anxious to trade with the Haida for the fur of the sea otter. These animals lived off the shores of the Queen Charlotte Islands. They had beautiful fur of long, silky, black hairs tipped with silver. The Haida hunted them to make cloaks which only the highest chiefs could wear.

The Europeans traded iron tools for sea otter pelts. Then, they took the pelts to China where sea otter fur was considered very valuable. There, the Europeans exchanged the pelts for tea, silk, and porcelain. They took these goods back to Europe and sold them for huge profits.

The fur trade went on for a number of years until there were almost no more sea otters. So, for a time, the Haida were part of a three-way trade route which went right around the world.

The European influence on the Haida way of life became stronger and stronger. As a result, the culture of the Haida began to change. For example, a Christian missionary arrived in 1876. He believed that the customs of the Haida were "heathen" practices. God, he said, would not approve of them. The missionary told the people to stop building totem poles. He threatened them with jail if they did not obey. He also told them that they had to live in European-style houses. He didn't like them living in the huge decorated houses that held many families.

This law was part of the *Indian Act*.

An event that especially damaged Haida culture occurred in 1884. The Canadian Government passed a law forbidding anyone to either hold or attend a potlatch. The Government disapproved of potlatches because they often left the Indians very poor. So the Haida were forced to give up a basic part of their culture.

Despite the law, many Haida continued to hold potlatches. But they had to keep them a secret. Then, in 1951, after years of complaints by both Indians and non-Indians, the Government changed its mind. The law against potlatches was removed from the *Indian Act*. The Haida could again continue their old customs in peace.

The Haida endured many other hardships after Europeans came. Epidemics of influenza and smallpox, diseases Europeans had brought with them, killed many Haida people. Settlers moved to the Haida's islands and took away much of their land. Haida children were sent away to schools where they were not taught their people's language and customs.

Before Europeans came, there were almost 10 000 Haida. By 1930, there were only two villages left, with only 650 Haida in all.

Despite the Government's ban on potlatches, the Haida continued to hold them, in secret. Blankets decorated with button designs were a popular gift.

Today, the Haida population is growing again. Now, there are almost 2000 people. Most of them make their living by fishing and working in lumber camps. Some are reviving the old art forms and becoming artists. Using the old styles, they are creating a new Haida art. This old and beautiful culture is beginning to rise again in new and modern forms.

7 The Inuit of the Arctic Region

Across the top of our planet lies the *Arctic* region, the "roof of the world." Canada's northernmost lands lie within this region. The Canadian Arctic stretches for 4800 km from the westernmost tip of the Yukon Territory to Labrador and Baffin Island in the east. It is a quiet and treeless land of tundra and icy seacoast.

This is the land of the Inuit. The word *Inuit* means "the people." (*Inuk* is the word for one person.) The Indians called them the *Eskimo*; it is an Algonkian word meaning "raw meat eaters." They themselves prefer the name *Inuit*. In this chapter, we will study their life.

Tundra is the treeless rolling plain lying along the Arctic Circle north of the tree line. The subsoil may be frozen year round. This permanently frozen ground is called permafrost.

The Inuit of the Western Arctic call themselves Inuvialuit, and their language, Inuvialuktun.

*   *   *

How and when did the Inuit first come to North America? Some archaeologists believe that the Inuit came to North America from northeast Asia about 3000 years ago, much later than the Indians. They probably crossed the Bering Sea by boat and landed in what is now called Alaska. From there, they gradually spread out across the Arctic as far east as Greenland. The idea that they came in one wave is supported by the fact that, across all the Arctic lands, the many groups of Inuit share a similar language and culture. They also have many cultural features in common with the Chuckchi and Koryak people of Siberia: round snowhouses, detachable harpoon heads, soapstone lamps, and the ulu, a moon-shaped knife.

However, others believe that the Inuit have been in North America much longer. They point to the mystery of remains of houses and tools which are more than 3000 years old. So the archaeological question of where the Inuit came from (and when) is still open.

INUIT OF THE ARCTIC REGION

The Inuit generally lived in the region north of the treeline.

The Arctic environment presented quite a challenge to the Inuit, especially the climate. Summers are short and cool, with an average temperature of 10°C. Winters are long and cold, with an average temperature of −30°C along much of the coastline.

The Inuit, however, knew how to keep warm in their cold climate. Their clothes provided them with almost complete protection. Indeed, their problem was not to become too hot. If they perspired, the moisture froze in their clothing and made it stiff and uncomfortable.

Inuit groups across the Arctic wore essentially the same kind of clothing. It varied only with the kinds of furs available. Both men and women wore knee-high sealskin boots called kamiks. Above these, they wore trousers of caribou hide or bearskin and a light shirt of hide. Sometimes the shirt was made of birdskin. It was worn with the feathered side turned inwards, rather like a feather T-shirt.

Over everything, the Inuit put on large, roomy parkas with the fur side against their skin. If it was very cold, they wore a second parka over the first, with the fur facing out. When they were all bundled up, it would have been hard to tell the men and women apart except for the style of their clothes. Men's parkas were cut straight at the bottom. Women's parkas had a long tail and a big pouch on the back in which to carry their babies.

Inuit clothing was so warm that it was like wearing a portable tent. In fact, when the people travelled, they often did not need to build overnight houses. They simply slept out in the open in their warm clothes. However, sometimes the Inuit had trouble keeping their hands and feet warm. If their boots became wet, or if they took their mittens off, there was the danger of frostbite.

The houses of the Inuit kept them warm in winter, too. Indeed, their houses were so warm that everyone, both adults and children, wore little or no clothing indoors.

Many people, when they think of Inuit houses, think of the snow house. Actually, the snow house was the main winter home only in the central Canadian Arctic. In the east, it was used mostly as a temporary shelter when travelling. In the west, it was hardly used at all. The winter home in these areas was made of stone walls, with a roof of driftwood covered with animal skins or sod.

The Inuit word igloo is commonly thought to refer only to the snow house. It actually refers to any Inuit house, whether made of snow or stone.

Whether made of snow or stone, the design of Inuit houses was basically the same. They were round-shaped, and usually there was a long entrance tunnel. The tunnel kept cold air from blowing in and was used for storage. Inside, almost half of the house was taken up by a large raised platform. It was used for sleeping and sitting. Heat in the house came from the people's bodies and from a stone lamp which burned fat.

In summer, the people lived in skin tents. They stayed in the tents until the cold forced them to move into their winter homes.

The Inuit invented many clever weapons and tools which helped them stay alive in the Arctic. For example, they had several kinds of spears and harpoons for hunting different mammals, fish, and birds. Special knives were used for skinning animals, for carving bone and ivory, for building snow houses, and for general purposes. There were also chisels, saws, drills, needles, needlecases, etc. — to list them all would take several pages. All of these were skilfully carved from wood, bone, ivory, or stone and were held together with pegs and sinews.

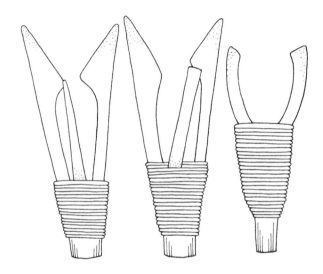

The Inuit skilfully carved harpoon heads like these from bone and ivory.

Most of the Inuit in Canada lived along the Arctic seacoast. The sea provided more food than did the inland plains. Many Inuit were experts in hunting such sea mammals as walrus, whales, and especially, seals.

In winter, the Inuit hunted seals through holes in the ice. Because a seal breathes air, it keeps several holes in the ice open. When a hunter found a hole, he placed a float in the water and sat down to wait. When the float bobbed, the hunter knew that a seal was coming up for air. He had to strike quickly with his harpoon. If he was slow, the seal might see him and escape.

In spring, seals like to lie on the ice and bask in the Arctic sun. Inuit hunters took advantage of this. They stalked the seals with harpoons, moving very slowly in order not to alarm them.

These two methods of seal-hunting took a great deal of patience. Often the hunt lasted many hours. And even then, there was a chance that the hunter would miss with his harpoon and go home empty-handed.

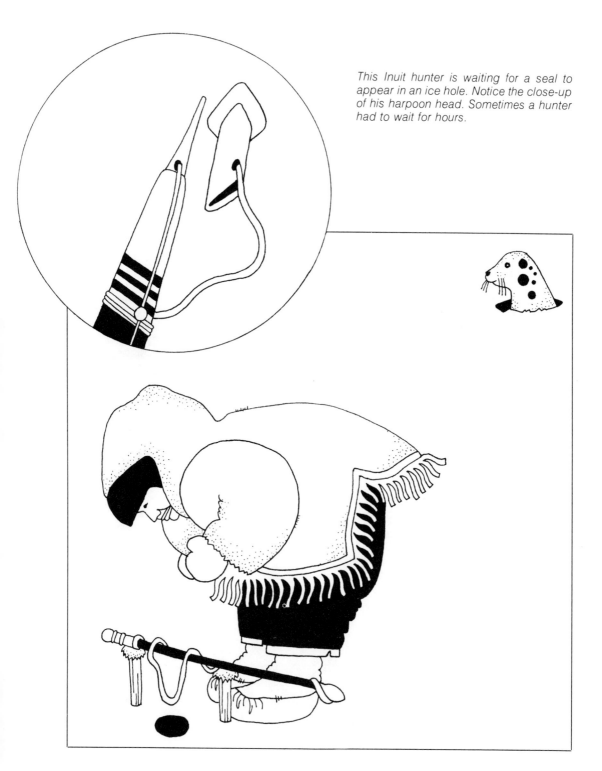

This Inuit hunter is waiting for a seal to appear in an ice hole. Notice the close-up of his harpoon head. Sometimes a hunter had to wait for hours.

One person could hunt a seal. But for bigger animals, such as walrus and whales, Inuit men had to work together.

Whales were hunted from a umiak, a large open boat. When a whale was sighted, brave Inuit hunters paddled up close and harpooned it. If possible, they also tried to cut the muscles in its flippers so that the whale could not strike out at the boat. Attached to the harpoon were air-filled floats. These made it difficult for the whale to dive and swim freely, and eventually caused it to tire out. Once the whale exhausted itself and came to the surface, the hunters killed it.

Whales were especially dangerous to hunt. One sweep of their flippers or tail could smash an umiak to pieces. However, they were considered worth the risk. The meat from one whale might feed a camp for several weeks.

In summer, the Inuit moved inland to hunt caribou. Vast herds of these deerlike animals migrated north every year. Their rumbling stomachs and their hooves clattering over the frozen tundra made a great deal of noise. The Inuit could hear them coming from far away. While the caribou were swimming across rivers, hunters in darting kayaks harpooned them. If there were no rivers nearby, the caribou were driven into corrals and killed with arrows.

The yearly caribou hunt was very important to the Inuit. As well as being a good source of meat, the caribou's skin made the best parkas — light, warm, and long-lasting.

Besides sea-mammals and caribou, the Inuit had many other sources of food. They made use of almost all the resources which the land could offer. They caught several kinds of fish, including whitefish, salmon, and char. They hunted birds, using bolas, and took eggs from the birds' nests. They also hunted smaller mammals such as hares and ground squirrels.

A kayak is a light, narrow boat that looks like a canoe but has an enclosed deck. A kayaker uses a paddle with a blade at each end and sits in a small opening in the deck, called a cockpit. The Inuit built their kayaks of sealskin or caribou skin stretched over a wooden or whalebone frame.

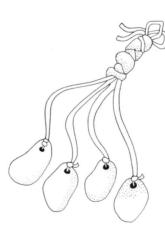

Bolas were made of stones tied together with leather thongs. When thrown accurately at a large bird, they wrapped around the bird's wings, causing it to fall to the ground.

The most dangerous animal the Inuit hunted was the polar bear. It was valued not only for its meat and fur, but also because hunting and killing it was considered a test of a man's courage. When a bear loomed out of the snow, a hunter released his dogs to chase and corner it. Once the bear had been distracted by the dogs snapping at its heels, the hunter moved in. He had to get close enough to throw his spear. If he was quick, he avoided the sweeping, claw-studded paws. Sometimes, however, the polar bear came out the winner.

Although the Inuit had many sources of meat, they had few sources of vegetables or fruit. Their most common source of vegetable food was partially-digested lichen from the stomach of the caribou. In summer, they found and ate plants such as seaweed or wild berries.

Whether they hunted alone or in groups, the Inuit almost always shared their catch with others. Only when the catch was too small to divide did they keep it for themselves.

Sharing, in fact, was one of the keys to Inuit culture. It was necessary to the survival of the group as a whole. Let's look at their situation to understand why.

Naturally, some Inuit men were better hunters than others. In a land of plenty, a poorer hunter might still manage to provide enough food for his family. In the Arctic, he probably couldn't. The line between survival and starvation was much too thin. And sometimes, no matter how good a hunter was, he still went home empty-handed.

By sharing, the Inuit made up for the difference between the skilled and the less-skilled hunter. They made certain that, as long as food was available, no one went hungry.

Sharing was done according to definite rules. For example, a hunter did not himself divide his catch among the group. Instead, a person whom everyone respected was chosen. The Inuit believed that this practice prevented anyone from feeling jealous or cheated. On the next page, you can see some of the rules for sharing animals.

Sharing was important for other things besides food. Inuit possessions were also shared. Often a person who needed something belonging to another simply took it, without asking for permission. The owner did not mind, for he or she knew that a borrower only took something that was really needed. Usually the borrowed object was returned sooner or later. But the owner never put a time limit on borrowing or pressed a person to return things.

The custom of borrowing often led to problems when Europeans began to live among the Inuit. If a hungry Inuk took a

European's gun to hunt for food, he was accused of stealing and the police were called. The Inuit did not understand this. To them, only a mean and selfish person would refuse to share with others.

The women also shared their skills. The work done by women was very important in the Arctic. A hunter who did not have a woman to care for him faced much difficulty. For example, the women made the warm, weatherproof clothing which protected the hunter from the cold. A man might mend his clothes if they were torn on a hunting trip. But he didn't know how to make a whole suit. So, if he went to visit a friend and left his wife behind, his friend's wife would take care of him. She would mend his clothes, feed him, and so on.

The Inuit child drawn below is using an ulu knife to cut up fish for drying. The Inuit kept their ulus very sharp.

Children were also shared. The Inuit loved children, and everyone felt sorry for a man and woman who had none. In fact, a couple who had several children often gave one to be adopted by a childless couple.

However, the Inuit did not share with everyone. Indeed,

These Inuit women are carving up sections of a whale. Using the numbers, notice who were given the different sections to eat.

1. **eyes** – dogs
2. **head** – men
3. **ribs** – everyone
4. **skin and blubber on belly** – women
5. **intestines** – dogs of the hunter(s) who killed it
6. **flippers** – everyone
7. **skin and blubber on back** –hunter's family
8. **back** – women

9. **skin and blubber of rear** – hunter who killed it
10. **tail** – everyone
11. **cloaca** – dogs
12. **heart** – men

strangers in camp might be considered enemies. Only if they could make friends with the people, or show that they were related to someone in the group, would they be treated with great hospitality.

Family relationships were another important part of Inuit society. It was considered a good thing to have as many relatives as possible. They could always be counted on for help. Marriage was an important way of joining two families.

The family was the basic governing body in Inuit society. It made all decisions about law and order, education, and caring for the sick. Relatives looked to the wisest person or the best hunter in their family group for leadership. If there was an important problem, everyone helped decide what to do.

Even though each family made their own decisions, different groups of Inuit across the Arctic generally agreed on what was right or wrong. The different groups shared a common set of beliefs and rules as part of their common culture. Some rules told people how they should behave towards each other. Other rules related to the animals they depended on for food and to the spiritual world.

The Inuit, like the Indians, believed that animals allowed themselves to be killed for the survival of the people. They also believed that each animal had a spirit and must be treated with respect. If its spirit was offended, it spoke to the spirits of all the other animals of its species. These animals would then refuse to allow any hunters to catch them.

A hunter, therefore, had to be on his best behavior. He had to use special charms and ceremonies to persuade the animal to come to him. He had to behave politely when the animal allowed itself to be killed. For example, the Inuit believed that sea mammals, because they lived in salt water, were always thirsty. So a hunter kept a mitten full of snow next to his body where it would melt. Then, when he killed a sea mammal, he could offer it a drink of fresh water.

To the Inuit, the world was a place where many forces were at work. There was little they could do to influence or change these forces. Instead, they tried to understand what the forces were, and how they could best live with them.

Catching a seal was certainly a matter of hunting skill and luck. But life in the Arctic was risky and catching a seal was very important. The Inuit didn't want to rely only on skill and luck. There was a world beyond that charms, ceremonies, and good behavior might reach. These, the Inuit believed, provided the help that might mean the difference between success and failure.

The Inuit Meet Europeans

The Inuit have been in contact with Europeans for a long time. It is possible that the first Europeans they saw were the Norse who occasionally travelled to North America. Certainly the Inuit in Greenland knew the Norse. The Norse had colonies there for many years.

After 1500 A.D., other European explorers travelled through the Arctic. They sought a northwest passage to the riches of China. This was what Henry Hudson was doing when he sailed into Hudson Bay in 1610.

In the 19th century, Europeans often visited the Arctic coasts to hunt whales. Sometimes, the Inuit traded with the sailors from the whaling ships. Other times, they fought with these strangers. They disliked Europeans for bringing diseases and for trying to kidnap their women and young men to work on board the ships. Whatever the case, occasional contact between the Inuit and the Europeans went on for many years.

The only places in the north where Europeans settled permanently were the trading posts of the Hudson's Bay Company. These posts extended around Hudson Bay and the Arctic. The Company traded with the Inuit for furs. They gave them guns, European foods, and clothing in return.

The fur trade began to affect the Inuit's traditional lifestyle. As the Inuit spent more time hunting for fur-bearing animals instead of food animals, they began to rely on European store-bought foods. These foods were not as nutritious as the foods the Inuit were used to eating. As a result, their health suffered. Many Inuit developed diseases such as tuberculosis, which are partly caused by poor diet.

The Inuit also began to use guns for hunting. Guns made hunting easier. No longer did a hunter have to stalk his prey for hours or run the risks involved in getting close enough to kill it. Many Inuit stopped making the traditional harpoons, spears, and bows and arrows.

Gradually the Inuit settled around the European stores. They grew to depend on trapping to buy European foods and supplies.

Today, some Inuit still support themselves by hunting. But others have never learned how to hunt. Even if they did, there is too little game around the towns where they live.

In order to be self-supporting, the Inuit have developed other sources of income. Their most successful business has been making soapstone carvings and prints and crafts for sale in the south. The Inuit artists and craft workers use many traditional skills in their work. They often show scenes from the old way of life.

Still, this business does not support everyone. More jobs are needed. Now, most companies in the north hire workers from the south. The Inuit leaders would like to see their own people hired and trained to fill these jobs.

Today, the Hudson's Bay Company runs stores in many Arctic settlements. Inuit people often work in the stores.

The Inuit organizations also want to run their own government and provide schooling that is suited to an Inuit way of life. These things they feel they can do. Their leaders hope that they will be given a chance to make a good life for themselves and everyone else in the north by following an Inuit way.

Today, there are about 100 000 Inuit in the world. About 25 000 live in Canada. The others live in Greenland, Alaska, and the eastern tip of Siberia. The Inuit in Canada have joined hands with the other Arctic peoples in the world to form the Circumpolar Conference — an organization which expresses their common purpose.

8 The Métis

There were no Métis in Canada before Europeans came. They are not a separate nation of Indians. The Métis are the children of mixed Indian and European ancestry. *Métis* is a French word, meaning "mixed-blood."

Métis people lived wherever Europeans and Indians met and married. The largest number of Métis in Canada, however, lived on the prairie. There, they developed a distinct culture. And, for a time, it seemed as though they would create their own state. This is their story.

*   *   *

The Métis of western Canada were the children of fur traders. Their fathers usually worked for either the British Hudson's Bay Company or for one of several companies based in Montreal. They brought their Indian wives to live at the trading posts. There, they raised their children.

When Métis boys grew up, many entered the fur trade. Some became hunters, trappers, or canoemen. Those with schooling became clerks or interpreters at the trading posts.

Gradually, as the Métis grew in number, they developed their own culture by combining Indian and European lifestyles. This culture appeared in many parts of Métis life. Let's look at some examples.

One example is dress. In winter, Europeans wore layers of heavy woollen clothing. Often, these clothes were so thick and heavy that moving became difficult. The Indians, however, dressed in straight flowing robes of leather which were light and easy to move around in. And they wrapped blankets around themselves for warmth. Métis women combined the leather of the Indian clothing and the tailoring styles of the European. They made leather jackets, pants, and coats which

Sometimes, a European father sent his Métis children back to his homeland to be educated.

A Métis man wore tailored clothes made of animal hides. They were decorated with beadwork and embroidery. Around his waist, he wore a "ceinture flêchée," a brightly-colored woven belt.

were both easy to move around in and warm. In fact, the Métis women became so good at this that they developed leather work into an art.

To decorate their clothes, the women bought glass beads from the trading companies. They sewed these on, using the designs their Indian mothers had once made with porcupine quills.

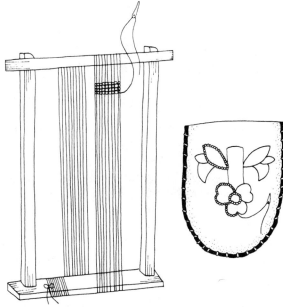

The Métis sometimes used a loom like this one to do beadwork. They also sewed beads onto leather using a needle and thread.

Another example is entertainment. The Métis loved to dance. They combined the intricate footwork of the Indians with Scottish and Irish reels and square dances. The new dance steps became known as the Red River Jig. For music, they used fiddles, favorite instruments of the Scots. However, imported European fiddles were very expensive. So the Métis made their own from maple wood and birch bark.

Métis dances often lasted several days, and are still popular today. Here is a description of a modern Métis dance.

Everyone would assemble at a particular home where all the furniture was removed and piled outside. The chairs and a small table were kept. The table served as the liquor bar and food stand. The only other piece of furniture kept was the stove. In summer this also would be removed. The preliminaries done, the dancing would commence with the men doing the toe-tapping (jigging). The women would then follow. Since many Métis who attended such dances were fiddle players, the dancing would often times continue for days on end or at least until liquor, food, and energy were all exhausted.

(Bruce Sealey, and Antoine S. Lussier, The Métis: Canada's Forgotten People [Winnipeg: Manitoba Métis Federation, 1975])

93

Carrioles are a type of
sleigh.

Horse-racing, a favorite sport of the Métis, also combined Indian and European customs. Horses were ridden by daring young men or were harnessed to gaily decorated carrioles. They were often seen dashing through the early western settlements. The Métis probably inherited their love of fast horses from the Plains Indians who prized them as swift buffalo-runners.

Even the economy of the Métis was mixed. Like European settlers, many Métis tended small farms. They kept a few animals and grew some vegetables and grain. However, every summer, they left to hunt the buffalo like their Indian kin.

Buffalo hunting became an important part of the Métis economy. They built it into a thriving business. The products of the hunt, especially pemmican, were sold to the fur companies.

Pemmican, made from dried buffalo meat, kept for months. Although tasteless, it was nutritious and compact. One kilogram of pemmican had the same food value as four kilograms of fresh meat. These qualities made it ideal for use in the fur trade. Fur traders and trappers could live on it when there was no fresh food around or not enough time to hunt.

Farming and hunting buffalo were two major sources of income for those Métis who were not directly employed by the fur companies. A third source was hauling goods to trading posts and settlements in Red River carts.

The design of the Red River cart came from France. However, instead of iron, the wheels were made from a piece of wood sawed from a tree trunk. The body of the cart was made entirely of wood, with the pieces bound together with rawhide. If a breakdown occurred, a nearby tree supplied the material for repairs. When a river barred the way, the wheels were simply removed and attached to the bottom of the cart. Then, the whole thing was floated across like a raft.

The carts had just one drawback. The noise they made was terrible. Early travellers said it sounded "as if a thousand fingernails were scraped across a thousand panes of glass." According to one Indian legend, the buffalo vanished from the prairie to escape the awful screeching noise made by the carts. The reason the carts were so noisy was because the wheels could not be greased. If they were, the grease would mix with the dust from the trails and cement the wheel to the axle. The drivers and their animals just had to get used to the shriek of grinding wood.

They did, and the carts became the foundation of land transportation in western Canada. Cart trails criss-crossed the prairie, linking various settlements. One well-worn trail went south from Red River (what is now Winnipeg) to St. Paul across the border in the United States. Another went as far west as Fort Edmonton. Indeed, many of western Canada's modern highways follow these old Red River cart trails.

For many years, the Métis lived by hunting, farming, freighting goods by Red River cart, or working for the fur companies. They were scattered in small groups across the prairie. Then, suddenly, a major change occurred. The cause of the change was the union of two large fur companies.

The most powerful traders in western Canada were the Hudson's Bay Company and the North West Company of Montreal. They competed fiercely. Sometimes there were even fights between their men. In 1821, the two companies decided to settle their differences. They joined together to become one company. It was called the Hudson's Bay Company.

As a result of the union, many Métis lost their jobs. Why? Almost every rich fur or pemmican area had two posts, one for each company. The new company needed only one post in each area. So it was left with too many employees.

The Red River carts used by the Métis were pulled by oxen.

The new Hudson's Bay Company wanted to help these people. It decided to help them become farmers. The Company offered to move them to Red River, just south of Lake Winnipeg. It agreed to provide the Métis with churches, schools, and grants of farmland. It also promised clothing, seeds, tools, and ammunition. Many Métis families accepted the offer and moved to Red River.

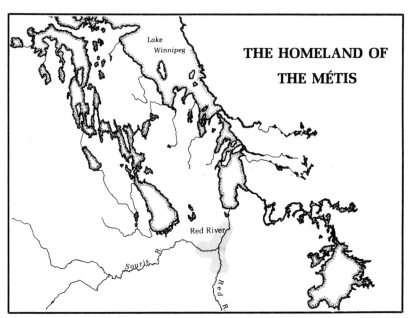

THE HOMELAND OF THE MÉTIS

Red River became the homeland of the Métis people. There, living together, they began to develop a sense of themselves as a distinct community. Churches and schools helped to make this happen. Catholic and Protestant missions were established at Red River. Until then, most Métis had followed the Indian religion of their mothers. At Red River, however, many became Christians.

The churches provided both education and leadership. When the Métis had been scattered across the prairie, it was difficult to provide schooling for their children. But, once most of them settled at Red River, a number of schools were started. Many Métis were trained as priests, missionaries, teachers, and scholars.

New Métis settlements spread out from Red River along the Red and Assiniboine rivers. The people of these settlements developed their own laws and government. They became a strong and united people. However, their strength was soon to be tested in what is often called the first Riel "Rebellion."

The Riel "Rebellions"

In 1867, the eastern provinces of Canada joined together in Confederation. In 1869, the Hudson's Bay Company agreed to sell its land in the northwest to the newly-formed Government of Canada. This land included the Red River area where the Métis were living. The Government wanted settlers from the east to move west to develop the land. It sent surveyors to map out the Red River area so that the land could be divided and sold. The Government planned to respect the Métis' existing land rights. But it did not tell them about its plan.

The Métis were angry that no one had consulted them about the sale of the Hudson's Bay Company's land. They were also afraid that the new Government would take away their rights, their way of life, and their land. They refused to allow any survey of their land and decided to take action against the Government. On December 10, 1869, they set up a provisional (temporary) government in Red River. It was led by an educated young Métis named Louis Riel.

The provisional government drew up a list of rights which they wanted the Canadian Government to guarantee. They wanted the right to elect an official government in Red River to take care of their affairs. They also wanted the right to elect members to the Canadian parliament in Ottawa. They wanted both French and English to be official languages in their own government, their own courts of law, and their schools. Finally, they wanted the Canadian Government to guarantee that they could keep all their existing "customs, privileges, and usages."

These demands showed that the Métis were simply concerned about preserving their culture. Also, they wanted to join Confederation of their own free will and with the right to vote.

Up to this point, the rebellion had been fairly quiet. Then, Riel made a move that created problems for him and the Métis for years to come.

The provincial government had put several men in jail for resisting Métis laws. One of these men was from Ontario. His name was Thomas Scott. Scott insulted the Métis and even threatened to destroy their government. Finally, the Métis government tried Scott in court. He was found guilty of disloyalty and of resisting Métis authority. On March 4, 1870, he was executed by firing squad.

Scott's death shook the faith of many of Riel's Red River supporters. In Ontario and Quebec, it created an uproar. There were demonstrations both for and against the Métis.

A rebellion is considered to be an illegal act of resistance against a government. Many people think that the Métis were legally right to set up their own government. The Hudson's Bay Company had given up its authority, and the Canadian Government had not yet taken over.

Indians, by contrast,
did not get the right to
vote until 1960.

However, the uprising had not been in vain. In 1870, the Government of Canada passed the *Manitoba Act.* It agreed to most of the demands in the list of rights the Métis had sent in Ottawa.

The uprising had forced the Government to listen to the protests of the Métis. The differences between the Métis and the rest of Canada seemed to be settled. The Métis joined Canada on terms which they felt would protect their culture and their rights.

However, the *Manitoba Act* did not protect Riel. When the Métis elected him to Parliament, he was not allowed to take his seat. Finally, the Government exiled him from Canada.

After Manitoba became a province of Canada, settlers flooded into Red River from the east. These newcomers did not always respect the Métis right to their lands. Often, when the Métis returned from buffalo hunting in the summer, they found that their land had been claimed. Sometimes, the settlers refused to give the land back.

Other conflicts developed between Métis and settlers. Many settlers had not forgotten the rebellion. Many disliked the Métis for being Catholic and part French and Indian. Fights broke out and some Métis leaders were beaten and killed. The Government did not want to take action. It was afraid that holding trials would create even more unrest.

To make matters worse for the Métis, the buffalo were moving farther west, away from the Red River area. Without the buffalo, many Métis would no longer be able to follow their old lifestyle. As a result, many Métis left Red River to follow the buffalo west. Some built settlements in other parts of Manitoba. Others spread out through present-day Saskatchewan and Alberta. They hoped that they would be safe in the western prairie and that they could follow their old way of life.

During the 1870s and early 1880s, many European settlers followed the Métis west. Once again, they started claiming Métis land. In despair, the Métis thought of their old leader, Louis Riel.

Riel was living in the United States. He had become an American citizen and was fighting for Métis rights in the state of Montana. When a number of Saskatchewan Métis asked him to return, he agreed to come back to help his people.

The first thing Riel did was to draw up a petition and send it to Ottawa. In it, he asked for four main things:
1. legal title to the land already occupied by Métis families
2. provincial status for the Districts of Saskatchewan, Assiniboia, and Alberta

3. laws to encourage the Indians and Métis to settle on farms
4. more liberal treatment of the Indians.

The government reply was a promise to consider the petition. The Métis, however, were not satisfied with this answer. So, once again, Riel set up a provisional government. This time, the Government in Ottawa responded by sending police to Duck Lake to arrest Riel. What followed was the first of several fights as the Métis tried to preserve their new government. Some Indians also joined the Métis. Eventually, they were all defeated by Government troops. Riel was captured and charged with treason.

A policeman and a Métis. The police were defeated by the Métis at Duck Lake. Eventually, however, Government troops claimed victory over the Métis forces.

Louis Riel, the Métis leader, went to school in Quebec. There he studied to become a priest.

Riel's trial created an uproar in Canada. Many people thought he was a madman and a traitor. Others thought he was a man with a mission to save his people's future. The court found Riel guilty and sentenced him to death. On November 16, 1885, he was hanged in the Mounted Police barracks at Regina.

In the next few years, the Canadian Government made an effort to solve some of the problems that had led to the Riel rebellions. They included the Métis in treaty negotiations.

100

Between 1885 and 1921, the Government signed treaties with the Indians. They were offered reserves. The Métis were given a choice. They could have either so much land per person, or scrip (a money coupon) worth anywhere from $160 to $240.

Many Métis remembered that they had not been able to keep the lands promised them in the past. So they chose the scrip. All too often, however, the money was quickly spent, and the people remained poor.

Today, many Métis still follow the same way of life as their forefathers and Indian kin. They live by hunting, fishing, and trapping. Some are farmers. Others have jobs in towns and cities.

The Métis share some of the problems that Indians face in Canada. For example, they tend to have little education. And about 70% speak a language other than English. Unlike Indians, however, they have no Canadian Government department to look after their interests. They have no reserves of their own, and they do not have such benefits as special hunting and fishing rights, free education, or medical care.

Today, the Métis are working together to solve these problems. They are using Government-paid programs to provide education and job training. In these efforts, they are helped by their organizations. Many Métis associations across Canada give leadership and assistance toward improving Métis life. They hope to do so while preserving as much of the Métis culture as possible.

A poem by Joel Anderson, a 10-year-old Métis from Manitoba, expresses his people's strength and purpose:

And now at the present
We have a lot of voice
So now, friends and brothers
Let us all rejoice
Because we're Métis. . .

We are Indian, we are white
We are rejected by them both
Although we are so lost between
We continue in our growth
As a Métis.

(Questions and Answers Concerning the Métis, [Winnipeg: Manitoba Métis Federation Press, 1973], p.13)

9 Contact With Europeans

Before Europeans came, Indians had lived in Canada for thousands of years. They may even have numbered 2.5 million in population. No one knows for sure. And there was almost no territory that one nation or another did not consider its own.

When Europeans arrived, they did not find an empty land. They found a land inhabited by people who considered it their home. A people who had their own customs, laws, and values.

The Europeans, however, brought different customs, laws, and values. Over time, they caused many changes in Indian life. Today, Indians tell a story which shows how they feel about this matter.

Some early writers thought there were as few as 220 000. However, new evidence shows that, in many areas, as many as ninety percent of the Indians died of diseases brought by Europeans. The old counts were probably based on survivors.

When the white man came, he found an Indian sitting on a log. "Move over," said the white man. So the Indian moved over and allowed the white man to sit on his log. But the white man was not happy. "Move over! Move over!" he kept demanding. Finally the Indian found himself sitting on the ground at the end of the log. Then the white man said, "Now this log is all mine!"

- Who were these Europeans who came to North America?

- What did they want?

- How did Indians and Europeans react to each other?

- How did the different ways of Europeans affect Indians?

In this chapter, we will consider questions like these.

The First European Visitors

The first European visitors were probably the Norse from Norway. We know that the Norse founded colonies in Iceland and Greenland. Their sagas (legends) also tell of a third colony on this continent. It was probably on the east coast, perhaps at L'Anse aux Meadows in Newfoundland. There, archaeologists have uncovered the remains of what they believe was a Norse village.

Norse sagas tell of the people the settlers met in North America. Here is a part of a saga. It describes how the two groups reacted to each other on first meeting.

> . . . early one morning when they (the Norsemen) looked about them, they saw nine skin-boats (canoes), on board which staves (paddles) were being swung which sounded just like flails threshing. . .
>
> "What can this mean?" asked Karlsefni.
>
> "Perhaps it is a token of peace," replied Snorri. "So let us take a white shield and hold it out towards them."
>
> They did so, and those others rowed towards them, showing their astonishment, then came ashore. They were small, ill favoured (dark) men, and had ugly hair on their heads. They had big eyes and were broad in the cheeks. For a while they remained there, astonished, and afterwards rowed off south past the headland.

(Gwyn Jones, The Norse Atlantic Saga [London: Oxford University Press, 1944])

According to the saga, the colony lasted only three years. The settlers fought with the Native people and were forced to abandon their settlement. However, the Norse continued to live in Greenland. They may have even continued to visit the east coast of Canada.

East coast Indians had probably met many Europeans by the time Jacques Cartier made his first voyage in 1534. Soon after 1500, fishermen from France and Portugal were sailing to the Grand Banks off Newfoundland. And a French explorer is reported to have taken some Indians back to France. Cartier, however, didn't just fish and go away, like the others. He claimed the land for France. Neither he nor the French Government recognized the Indians' claim to the land.

At first, Europeans were more interested in fishing than in settlement. Because of poor farming methods and a shortage of meat in Europe, the French needed North American fish.

The Indians offered friendship to the first Europeans.

Fishermen and Indians seldom met, except when the fishermen came ashore to dry their fish before sailing home.

This situation lasted for many years. Then, in the early 1600s, beaver hats came into fashion in Europe. There were not enough beaver in Europe to fill the demand. In North America, however, beaver were plentiful. So the French decided to establish a fur trade with the Indians there. They sent settlers to start a colony.

The French preferred to have the Indians collect the furs because they were better trappers. They persuaded Indians to spend the winter trapping beaver. In summer, the Indians brought the rich, brown pelts to the French trading posts.

This arrangement suited the Indians. It helped them get European trade goods, which made their lives easier. Metal arrowheads, knives, axes, and kettles were much stronger and longer lasting than stone tools and bark containers. The Indians also liked French beads and cloth, which added bright color to their skin clothing.

The European trade goods that Indians got from trading posts, like the one drawn here, helped to make their lives easier.

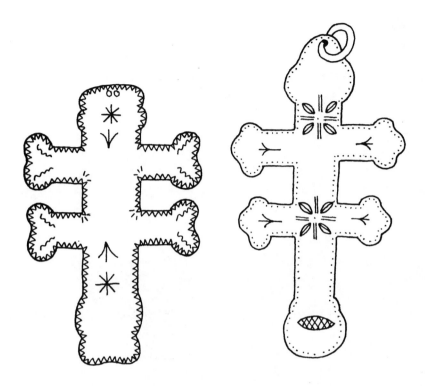

The French in Quebec made ornaments from silver to trade to the Indians. Indians loved the ornaments. A wealthy chief might wear up to 15 kg of the trade silver.

Perhaps the Indians found trading easy to accept for another reason, too. The French were not much interested in settling on the land. There was much unused farm land in France, so they saw no need to move all the way to North America to farm. Only a few came to stay. However, even though they did not settle the land, the French still considered it their own.

The French were not the only Europeans in Canada at this time. The British were also trading in the far north. In 1670, a group of them started the Hudson's Bay Company. The British Government gave the Company the sole right to trade in the lands drained by rivers flowing into Hudson Bay. It was a huge territory and included most of northern and western Canada.

Like the French in the south, the Hudson's Bay Company was interested in trade, not settlement. It encouraged the Indians to continue a life of trapping fur-bearing animals.

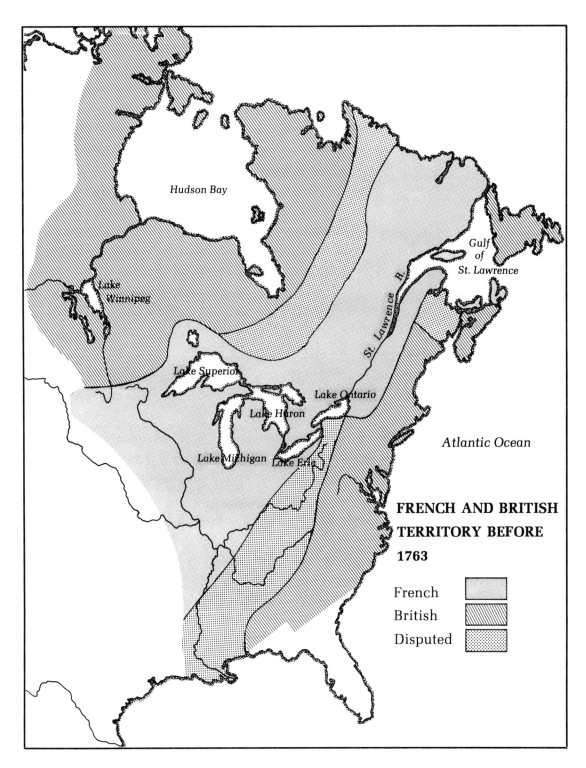

Hudson Bay

Gulf
of
St. Lawrence

Lake
Winnipeg

Lake Superior

St. Lawrence R.

Lake Ontario

Lake Huron

Atlantic Ocean

Lake Michigan

Lake Erie

FRENCH AND BRITISH

TERRITORY BEFORE

1763

French

British

Disputed

Sudden Changes in Indian Life

In 1759, the British defeated the French after a long war. Much of Canada became part of the British Empire. However, this brought few changes to the Indian way of life. They continued trading furs as before.

Then, in 1776, Britain's thirteen colonies in America rebelled. Britain lost the war with its colonies and the United States was formed. Many former colonists in the United States still wanted to live under British rule. So they moved north to British territory. Most of them settled in the lands now known as Ontario, Quebec, and the Atlantic provinces of Nova Scotia, New Brunswick, and Prince Edward Island. The European population of Canada increased from 90 600 in 1776 (mostly French living in Quebec) to 520 000 by 1812.

The British Government encouraged this northward movement because it feared another war with the United States. It wanted as many loyal settlers as possible to defend its remaining colonies in North America. To persuade settlers to come, the Government offered generous grants of land.

Several Indian nations also moved to Canada. The Iroquoian-speaking Six Nations had long lived in what, after 1776, became New York State. They fought for the British during the war of independence. Afterwards, the British gave them land in Ontario and Quebec in reward for their help. In 1792, a group of Delaware Indians came to Canada. The Indians had been converted to Christianity, and brought their missionaries with them. Another group, the Muncey Indians, followed in 1795.

In 1816, thousands more settlers began to arrive from Britain. The British Government had just finished yet another war with France. It no longer needed its large army. So it had to find work for many unemployed soldiers. The Government decided to offer them free land in Canada. Many accepted eagerly.

As time went by, more and more people left Britain. Besides soldiers, many were people left unemployed due to changes in farming and industry. We learn about their hopes from Susannah Moodie, herself one of the immigrants.

> From the year 1826 to 1829, Australia and the Swan River were all the rage. No other portions of the habitable globe were deemed worthy of notice. . . . In 1830, the great tide of emigration flowed westward. Canada became the great landmark for the rich in hope and poor in purse. Public newspapers and private letters teemed with the unheard-of advantages to be derived from a settlement in this highly-favoured region. . . .

The Six Nations, also called the Iroquois Confederacy, was made up of six independent nations. They were the Mohawk, Oneida, Onondaga, Cayuga, Seneca, and Tuscarora.

There were a few other changes in Indian populations. In the late 1700s, the Gros Ventre of the prairie moved south. In the 1830s, some Potawatomi moved to Ontario. In the 1870s, the Sioux, led by Sitting Bull, fled to Canada to escape the U.S. cavalry. Most of them returned to the United States, but a large group stayed in Canada.

The infection became general. A Canada mania pervaded the middle ranks of British society; thousands and tens of thousands, for the space of three or four years, landed upon these shores.

(Susanna Moodie, Roughing It In the Bush [Toronto: McClelland and Stewart, 1962])

So, in the short space of fifty years, eastern Canada changed from a place where Europeans were seldom seen to a land dotted with their towns and villages. The Indians had to adjust very quickly to the flood of settlers. It was not an easy change to make.

Most of the new settlers had no interest in the fur trade. Instead, they wanted to clear the land of its forests so they could farm. They also wanted ownership of the land they cleared.

The settlers saw no place for Indians in this scheme. The Indians occupied or claimed ownership of much of the land that the settlers wanted to use. They insisted on using the land for hunting and fishing. The settlers considered this a waste of good farm land. They felt that the Indians were standing in the way of progress.

The Making of Treaties

In legal language, this practice of treaty and payment was called "extinguishing" the Indians' claims to ownership.

The British Government undertook to solve the ownership problem. It persuaded the Indians to give up their rights to the land and settle down on reserves. The Government also hoped to persuade them to give up hunting and become farmers. So, it began to make treaties with the Indians. By signing the treaties, the Indians gave up their rights to the land. In return, they were given money and such gifts as farm equipment and animals. The treaties also guaranteed that the reserve lands belonged to the Indians forever.

Why did the British Government bother with treaties instead of just taking the land? The British recognized that the Indians had a right to the land. Indians were, after all, the first people to live in North America. So British settlers could not own the land until agreement had been made with the Indians. Also, some kind of payment had to be made.

The first treaty was signed in 1725. The last was signed in 1923. In all, there were about 500 separate treaties. Most concerned fairly small parcels of land. A few were for huge tracts.

The largest surrenders of land were made through a series of treaties called the "numbered treaties" — Treaties One to Eleven. They were signed between 1871 and 1921. By these eleven treaties, the Indians surrendered what are now the

It often took days of hard bargaining before treaties were signed. The chiefs wanted to be sure that their people's rights were protected under the terms of the treaties.

provinces of Manitoba, Saskatchewan, and Alberta, and parts of Ontario, British Columbia, and the Northwest Territories.

Look at the sample of one treaty, Treaty Number Four. Notice who the treaty was made with and what the promises were.

Even though so many treaties were signed, large areas of Canada were never negotiated. For example, much of Quebec, British Columbia, and the Northwest Territories, the Yukon, and the Atlantic provinces were never legally surrendered.

After the treaties were made, the Government decided that the Indians should gradually learn to live like Europeans. So it created a special policy. It expected the Indians to settle down on the reserves and become farmers and ranchers.

AN EXAMPLE OF A TREATY

Treaty Four
September 15, 1874. Made with the Cree, Salteaux and others.
Area given up: mainly southern Saskatchewan; 193,203 km²

Indian Promises
- To observe the treaty
- To maintain peace
- To not molest persons or property
- To assist in bringing Indian offenders to justice

Government Obligations
- To set aside reserves of 2.6 km² per person, subject to government rights to deal with settlers on reserve lands
- To sell or rent lands on the reserves, so long as money for improvements or land is given
- To provide schools
- To give the Indians the right to hunt, trap, or fish as long as they obeyed government laws
- To control liquor traffic

Treaty Presents
- Indians, $12; chiefs, $25; headmen, $15
- miscellaneous agricultural equipment, supplies, etc.
- flags and medals
- Annuities (to be paid every year): Indians, $5; chiefs, $25; headmen, $15
- $750 every year for ammunition and twine
- Suit of clothes for chiefs and headmen every three years

The Government's policy was called a policy of "assimilation." They wanted to "assimilate" Indians, to make them live like Europeans.

It was hoped that the reserves would only be needed for a short time, just until the Indians forgot their old way of life. Then, they could be broken up and the Indians merged with the general population. To help make this happen, the Canadian Government passed the *Indian Act* in 1876. It defined who was a legal Indian and what could be done with the reserves. Also, a special branch of Government, called the Department of Indian Affairs, appointed Indian agents all across Canada. The agents were responsible to look after the Indians' interests and teach them to become settlers.

112

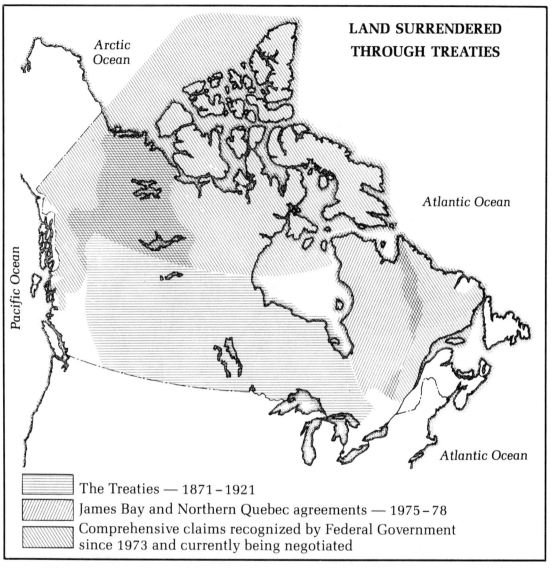

LAND SURRENDERED
THROUGH TREATIES

Arctic Ocean

Atlantic Ocean

Pacific Ocean

Atlantic Ocean

The Treaties — 1871–1921

James Bay and Northern Quebec agreements — 1975–78

Comprehensive claims recognized by Federal Government since 1973 and currently being negotiated

At first, the Government's policy was not very successful. Many Indians left their reserves to continue hunting and trapping. They only returned at certain times of the year to collect their treaty payments. However, except in northern Canada, the situation gradually changed. Settlers cleared the land around the reserves and put up fences. As a result, much of the wildlife disappeared. The buffalo — the backbone of life for the Indians and the Métis in the west — were almost wiped out. Without the animals, Indians were forced to find other ways of making a living.

Lands set aside for Indians are called "reserves" in Canada. In the United States, they are called "reservations."

Before Europeans arrived, Indians had controlled their own lives. They fed and clothed themselves. They ran their own government. They had their own religion. And they had their own ways of teaching their children. Also, there was no such thing as unemployment. When something needed doing, such as gathering food, they simply did it. If there was nothing important to do, then they relaxed. Perhaps they took the time to play games or tell stories to their children.

Now, Indians were told to forget their religion and become Christians. The *Indian Act* even banned some of their religious customs. They were also told that their children must go to school. Often, children were taken away from their parents to live in boarding schools for years at a time. They were forbidden to speak their own languages and were punished if they did. They had to learn to speak English. And they learned little or nothing about their own culture.

Government among Indians ceased to be a matter of the people following a leader who made good decisions. Instead, they were told that they must elect a chief and a band council. As it turned out, a chief and council had little real power. Important decisions were made by the Department of Indian Affairs in Ottawa, and by the local Indian agent.

The Christian churches ran boarding schools for Indian children. The children learned about European culture but were not taught about their own culture.

Making laws and punishing offenders were taken over by the police and courts. The customary laws that Indians had followed for hundreds of years no longer applied. They had to live under laws made by Europeans. Even if they had no idea what these laws were.

Indians adapted as best they could to the European way of living. In southern Canada, many became farmers and ranchers. In the north, many became miners, trappers, guides, and fishermen. In British Columbia, many worked in logging camps and on salmon fishing boats. On the east coast, many worked in the lumber industry and in shipbuilding. Throughout Canada, the women contributed by making crafts for sale — needlework, beaded moccasins and jackets, basketry, and tourist souvenirs.

The jobs Indians chose at least allowed them to stay on the land and use the skills they had. Still, many of these jobs were in boom-or-bust industries, good one year, bad the next. So when there was no work, or when the land was not good for farming, they were left unemployed.

Many Indians found themselves caught between two cultures, the old and the new. Which should they follow? It was a hard choice to make.

10 Modern Issues

Indians, Inuit, and Métis altogether are known as Native people. There are at least one million people in Canada with Native ancestry. This is almost five percent of the total Canadian population.

In the Northwest Territories, Native people are the majority population — seventy percent. In the Yukon Territory, they make up twenty-five percent of the population. In Saskatchewan, they form about ten percent. In some provinces, they form large groups. In fact, the largest numbers of Native people live in Ontario and British Columbia.

Canada's Native population is growing rapidly. Their birthrate (the number of children born) is twice as high as the Canadian average. So, in the future, Natives may form an even larger part of the Canadian population.

Officially, Native people are divided into three main groups: status Indians, Inuit, and Métis and non-status Indians.

Status Indians are sometimes called registered or treaty Indians. The *Indian Act* defines a status Indian as a person registered by the Government as an Indian. Their names are kept on a list in Ottawa. Each person is given a number. Children use their fathers' number until they grow up. Then, they are given their own number.

The first lists were made many years ago. Some were made when Indians signed treaties. Indian agents registered the Indians who did not sign treaties. In 1957, a final list was made. In most cases, only people whose families were on it can be registered as Indians today.

There are only two ways non-registered people can become status Indians. One way is to prove that their families should have been on the list. This is usually very hard to do. The other way is for a woman to marry a status Indian man. Then the woman (Native or non-Native) becomes a status Indian, as do her children. But status Indian women lose their status if

Throughout this section, Government refers to the Federal Government, unless otherwise noted.

117

they marry non-registered men. Many Indian women feel this is unfair, and are trying to change the law.

There are about 300 000 status Indians in Canada today. They are the people usually counted as Indians in Government figures and reports.

The second group of Native people is the Inuit. For a long time, the Government did not recognize the Inuit as legally Native. Then, in 1939, the Supreme Court decided that Inuit were "Indians" according to the *British North America Act*. This meant that the Federal Government was responsible for them. However, the *Indian Act* still does not apply to Inuit.

There are about 25 000 Inuit in Canada today. Most live in the north beyond the tree line.

The two groups of people who are legally Native — status Indians and Inuit — receive special services from the Government. The Department of Indian and Northern Affairs is responsible for them. It pays for programs in health, education, social services, and various other matters.

The third group of Native people is formed by the Métis and non-status Indians. They are the people who are not legally Indian, but have Native ancestry. Nobody knows exactly how many people make up this group. There may be as few as 300 000 or as many as 750 000. So far the exact number has been counted only in the Yukon Territory and the Northwest Territories.

When treaties were made and Indians were being registered, the Métis were not counted as Indians (Sometimes treaties provided land or money for the Métis because of their partial Indian ancestry.). They are the only Native group in Canada who have never been legally registered.

Non-status Indians, on the other hand, are people whose families were once status Indians. Either their familes or they themselves lost their Indian status. There are several ways in which this could happen. Until 1951, the *Indian Act* did not allow status Indians to vote, hold public office, or run businesses. Those who wanted to do these things had to give up their status. Indian women and their children lost their status by marrying non-status men.

Many Métis and non-status Indians have the same needs and desires as status Indians. For example, they wish to keep their culture alive. However, the government does not give them the same rights as status Indians. They do not have reserve lands of their own. And they can't get money for such services as education or housing from the Department of Indian Affairs in Ottawa.

Native People and the Land

Some Native people in Canada live on reserves. Today, there are about 2200 reserves, each varying in size. Some are tiny. The Whitesand Reserve in Ontario, for example, is only .2 ha. Others are huge. The Blood Reserve in southern Alberta is one of the largest — 1436 km². Some reserves are located in the middle of cities. A Squamish band occupies land in North Vancouver. Other reserves are far from the cities. They can only be reached by airplane or canoe.

The majority of Native people do not live on reserves. This is the case with the Inuit and almost half of all status Indians. They have no reserves because they have never signed treaties with the Government. The Métis and non-status Indians have no reserves, either. So where do they live?

The Métis, non-status Indians, and status people without reserves, are widely-scattered. Some live in cities, some on farms, and some in the bush. In western Canada, some Métis live in settlements called "Métis colonies." They were formed by provincial governments in this century. They are lands set aside for Métis people. There are many settlements where Métis and Indians live side by side. They are in British Columbia and in the north, especially the Yukon and Mackenzie River valleys.

Sometimes, treaties provided land or money for the Métis because of their partial Indian ancestry.

Until recently, the Inuit were scattered across the north in small hunting camps. In the 1950s, the Government persuaded them to move into settlements. Then, their children could attend school. Inuit settlements now dot the Arctic coastline. They are small settlements of brightly-painted houses — blue, green, and purple — perched on rocky hills looking out over the ocean. Sometimes, sled dogs can be seen curled up beside the houses. More often, a snowmobile is parked outside the door.

Those Native people who never signed treaties are concerned about their land rights. The old British view was that Native people had rights to the land. These rights continued until signed away through treaty and payment. Native people who never signed treaties insist that their rights still exist.

The question of Native rights to the land has become urgent in places where development is planned. Native people feel responsible for the land. They are concerned about how it will be used. They fear that mines, roads, and pipelines will disturb the natural environment. They worry that they and their children will not be able to hunt and fish as their ancestors did.

In legal language, Native people's right to the land is called "aboriginal title."

119

The feelings of Native people go beyond questions of legal rights or economics. To them, the land is the source of all life. They wish to preserve it for future generations. As Isadore Kochon of Colville Lake explained:

> This land fed us all even before the time the white people ever came to the North. To us it is just like a mother that brought her children up. That's how we feel about this country.

And as Gabe Bluecoat of Arctic Red River remarked:

(Thomas R. Berger, Northern Frontier, Northern Homeland: The Report of the Mackenzie Valley Pipeline Inquiry, Volume 1 [Ottawa: Supply and Services, 1977])

> The land, who made it? I really want to find out who made it. Me? You? The government? Who made it? I know [of] only one man who made it — God. But on this land who besides Him made the land? What is given is not sold to anyone. We're that kind of people. What is given to us, we are not going to give away.

For a long time, the Canadian Government has insisted that aboriginal rights no longer exist. In 1969, Prime Minister Trudeau gave a speech in Vancouver. He agreed that the Indians had been badly treated in the past. But whoever was right or wrong, he said, aboriginal rights belonged to the past. The Government would not re-open the question. In his exact words:

> If we think of restoring aboriginal rights to the Indians well what about the French who were defeated at the Plains of Abraham? Shouldn't we restore rights to them? And what about the Acadians who were deported — shouldn't we compensate for this?. . . What can we do to redeem the past? I can only say . . . We will be just in our time. This is all we can do.

Then, in 1973, the Nishga Indians caused the Government to change its mind. The Nishga live in the Nass River valley of northwestern British Columbia. They have never signed a treaty giving up their title to the land. Since 1913, they have been petitioning the Government to recognize their title. In 1973, they asked the Supreme Court to judge their claim. Although some of the judges agreed with the Nishga claims they lost the case. But they did win strong legal support for Native rights.

Of the seven judges, three voted for the Nishga claim, and three against. The seventh judge voted no on a technical point. He said the Nishga's lawyer did not follow proper procedure in bringing the case to court.

As a result, the Government began negotiating to settle other land claims. Discussions of claims started in the Northwest Territories, the Yukon Territory, British Columbia, Quebec, Labrador, and the Maritime provinces of Nova Scotia, New Brunswick, and Prince Edward Island.

Many Indians and Inuit want more than payment for their land. They want to have a say in how the land will be used, now and in the future. They insist that commercial and industrial development be postponed until this matter is decided.

Those Canadians who support development disagree. They feel that their projects will benefit all Canadians. They will create jobs and make money. They argue that these benefits should not be delayed because of the rights of small numbers of Native people.

In 1974, Judge Thomas Berger presided over an inquiry into the building of the Mackenzie Valley pipeline project. He listened to what the people in the villages along the Mackenzie River had to say.

In 1978, the Naskapis of Shefferville in northern Quebec signed a similar agreement.

Only one Native land claim has been settled so far. It concerns the James Bay area of northern Quebec. The provincial government wanted to build a huge hydro-electric power project. So, the Cree and Inuit who lived in the area were asked to give up their title to the land. They said yes, and a final agreement was reached in 1975.

Elsewhere, talks are still going on. But they take a long time. To Indians and Inuit alike, it seems that the Government does not really want to settle their claims. Some think Ottawa just wants to go on talking forever. Why the delay? The Government replies that more planning is needed. It says that different Native groups claim the same land, and this has to be sorted out. Perhaps the Government feels that Native people are asking too much. One official estimate is that it will cost 4.5 billion dollars to settle all the claims. So, making decisions on Native land claims is likely to be a long and expensive process.

Cree chief, Billy Diamond, signed the James Bay Agreement. Judd Buchanan, then Minister of Indian Affairs, and Robert Bourassa, then premier of Quebec, looked on.

Native Culture: Continuity and Change

Before Europeans arrived, Native people lived comfortably off the land. They made their own laws, and freely practised their traditional customs and habits. After Europeans arrived, however, Native people had to adjust quickly to many changes. As a result, they began to lose control of their lifestyles. This led to hardship and, in many cases, poverty. Let's look at some examples.

One example is jobs. In many places in Canada, Native people tried to farm. However, they were often given land that settlers didn't want. Either the soil was poor, the climate harsh, or both. Sometimes, they were given good farm land. Indian farmers of southern Ontario, for example, often won prizes at county fairs for their crops and livestock. However, these farms were small and made little money.

For a long time after Europeans arrived, Native people continued to live by trapping. This provided a good living while fur-bearing animals were plentiful. But when settlement spread and reduced their numbers, fewer Indians could make a living this way.

Other sources of income have been open to Natives, such as fishing, picking wild rice, making crafts, and fighting forest fires. However, some of these jobs are seasonal. They provide income for only part of the year.

Not all Native people in Canada are poor. In fact, some are well off, just as some non-Native people are. They are successful business people, construction workers, lawyers, doctors, teachers, and professors. But these people are few in number. Most of Canada's Native population face unemployment. For example, almost 50 percent of status Indians have no jobs for part of the year. And on some reserves, up to 95 percent of the people are unemployed during the winter.

Another hardship Native people face is inadequate housing. Many of their houses are small and yet are home to large families. They are often poorly insulated against winter's cold. And many have no plumbing or running water. Most Canadians take these things for granted.

Yet another hardship of Native people is poor diet. They often eat only cheap, prepared foods. These are high in starch and sugar but have little of the proteins or vitamins needed for good health. Many Native people seldom eat fresh meat, fruit, or vegetables. These usually cost too much money, especially in remote areas where shipping costs are high. Where they can, Native people try to improve their diet by hunting, fishing, and growing their own vegetables. But in many places where they live, the growing season is short and game is scarce. And often, lakes are polluted, making it dangerous to eat the fish.

Together, inadequate housing and poor diet lead to bad health. Tuberculosis, for example, is still a problem. However, Native people are no longer exposed to epidemics of such diseases as smallpox, typhus, and cholera. But in some parts of Canada, the death rate among Native children is well above the Canadian average.

Sometimes, Native people try to overcome these hardships by moving to cities. There, they hope to find work, better housing, and other services. But many lack the skills city jobs require. They may be expert hunters or fishermen, but this is no training for city work. Often, they do not have as much schooling as employers demand. And many do not speak English well, especially if they come from the north where Native languages are still commonly used.

Friendship centres, run by Native people, help many who come to cities. The centres help find jobs, run sports and games, and give advice.

It's a gloomy picture, but not as bad as it once was. Native people all over Canada are working together to help their people. They are starting businesses where Native people live. The Pas band in Manitoba, for example, has built a shopping centre. It employs several hundred band members. People come from all over to shop there.

Native people are also reviving their traditional self-government. In this way, they hope to provide better services for their communities. At James Bay, for example, the Cree and Inuit have set up regional councils. They run their own schools and other public services. The Inuit in the Northwest Territories want to make their own laws and have other powers of government. They have proposed that the eastern Arctic become a province. They will call their province Nunavut, which means "our land."

These changes alarm some non-Natives. They are afraid that Canada will be divided into blocks of Natives and non-Natives. They also fear that, if given power, Natives will treat them unfairly. As a result, many non-Natives argue that Native people are not yet ready to control their own affairs. They say they need more training and experience. What do you think?

Besides the hardships of daily life, Native people are constantly concerned about preserving their traditional customs and habits, their cultural heritage. Their heritage is very important to them. By providing a link with the past, it gives them an identity.

In the past, Europeans tried to make Native people give up their old ways. While Native people resisted these attempts,

124

Today, pow-wow dances bring together Indians from all over Canada. It takes much practice to learn the dance steps. One skill required is to be able to stop dancing the moment the drums stop.

much change went on anyway. New developments in technology, like airplanes and television, especially affected their lives. Today, Native people are trying to control this process of change.

One important way of doing this is by education. Native teachers are teaching in Native schools so that children can learn from people who understand their heritage. In some

Indians used to chew the leaves of wintergreen, an evergreen herb, as a cure for headaches. Now, doctors have learned that wintergreen contains the same ingredients as some modern headache tablets.

schools, teaching is even done in Native languages. And elders sometimes come into the classrooms to tell children stories of the past and to teach traditional skills.

Native culture is being preserved in other ways, too. For example, traditional medicines are being used again. Native people know many remedies made from plants. Doctors are finding that some of these cures work well.

Some people follow Native religions and spiritual beliefs. These beliefs teach how to live in harmony with the land. They developed over centuries as Native people came to understand the spiritual forces in nature.

Many Native people still use traditional medicines made from wild plants.

Native artists, sculptors, writers, and craft workers are creating many beautiful works. They enrich Canadian society with their interpretations of their very old, distinct cultures. Some of the most famous Native artists are Norval Morrisseau and Carl Ray from northern Ontario, Bill Reid and Tony Hunt from British Columbia, and Kenoujuak and Pitseolak from Cape Dorset.

The following items used in Canadian society today were first developed by Native people.

Foods	Transport	Crafts	Clothes
corn	canoe	quillwork	moccasins
beans	kayak	beadwork	mukluks
squash	toboggan	moosehair	parka
maple syrup	snowshoes	embroidery	

The questions of Native heritage and identity are difficult ones. Native people themselves do not always agree on what they mean. Native identity is something that each person must resolve as best as he or she can. Here are the opinions of three young Native people who were students in law school.

You have to have a good grasp of your own identity before you can move in the white society. The way I see it, it's like going down the river in separate boats; you're in the same stream, but you're moving with different currents. (A Métis from Manitoba)

When I entered law school, I was full of anger. For a long time, I rejected my own culture. I thought it was at the bottom end of white culture.

Now I realize that there are two completely different continuums (paths). Indians are on a completely different one. A lot of young Indians don't realize this. They think they're at the bottom and therefore they're bitter.

Indian people have to learn to understand what the white culture and the Indian culture are, and how the two may be reconciled. (A Cree from Saskatchewan)

The cultural barrier is a mental block. Culture is an emotional thing. It prevents you from spreading your wings and trying new things. You have to step over it in order to succeed.

A person makes that step by his willingness to set aside some of the things he learned in his own community and accept the new. Our elders say not to do that, but you have to. (An Indian from British Columbia)

Organizing for the Future

The situation of Native people is not only a question for themselves. It concerns non-Natives as well. In the past, most non-Natives saw Native people as a problem. They were "savages" to be feared, or "primitive" people to be pitied. The matter of dealing with them was left up to the Government and the churches. The non-Native public did not often concern itself with what was going on.

Seldom did Native people receive any recognition. What little they did get was for the kinds of success that non-Natives admired among themselves. For example, the Mohawk poet, Pauline Johnson, was highly regarded. So was the marathon runner, Tom Longboat. And so were those who fought for their country — Joseph Brant, Tecumseh, as well as hundreds of Native men who distinguished themselves during two World Wars.

A turning point came in 1969. The Government published a paper called "Indian Policy." It proposed to end special status for Indians and transfer responsibility for them to the provinces. In effect, they would have the same rights, duties, and privileges as other citizens. But they would lose most special rights as Indians.

All over the country, Native people reacted quickly. They joined together, forming organizations to fight the proposal. They began to discuss exactly what rights they wanted and made many counter-proposals to the Government. Issues that had simmered for more than a hundred years came to a boil. Some of these were land rights, treaties, the *Indian Act*, self-government, education, religion, and the preservation of Native heritage.

The events surrounding the "Indian Policy" paper sparked an explosion of Native concerns in the 1970s. Native people were constantly in the newspapers. Some were picketing, demonstrating, or organizing marches. Others wrote proposals.

The 1970s were a time of revolution for Canada's Native people. Perhaps many of the concerns raised during this time will lead to solutions in the years to come.

The future belongs to us all, Native and non-Native. What will it bring? This will depend in part on the attitudes of non-Native Canadians. Native people must not be seen as a "problem." Their culture should not be ignored. Rather, Canadians should learn to appreciate Native culture.

Young Native people sometimes organize peaceful demonstrations. They want to see their people assume their rightful role in society. By standing together, they feel, they can accomplish this goal.

The Ojibwa tell an old story. Eight fires would come to the Indian people. Each would bring great changes to the peoples' lives. Ojibwa prophets foretold what the fires would be like.

The first three fires were early in Ojibwa history. The fourth prophet told of the coming of the Europeans, called *zhagonosh* in Ojibwa. The fifth warned that there would be a great struggle between the Indians and the zhagonosh. The sixth prophet said that the Indian children would turn against their elders. They would forget their history. The Indian ways would almost disappear. The seventh prophet spoke of a time when the zhagonosh would be given a choice for all the nations of Canada.

The seven prophets were preparing the way for an eighth and last fire still to come. They said that the chiefs and mede would not be able to control this fire.

What happened would depend on the choice made by the zhagonosh. It could be a fire of destruction. The fire could turn back on its makers when the wind changed. Or it could be an everlasting fire of peace, love, and brotherhood.

Important Dates

Listed below are some important dates in the history of Canada's Native people. Many are mentioned in this book.

B.C.	c. 63 000	last ice age began
	c. 60 000–20 000	Indians come to North America
	c. 8600	Indians at Camp Debert in Atlantic coast region
	c. 8000	end of last ice age
	c. 5500	woolly mammoth and other big game die out
	c. 5000–2000	corn, beans, and squash developed in Mexico
	c. 1000	Inuit come to North America
A.D.	c. 800–1000	Norse come to North America
	c. 1000	corn reaches Huron in Ontario
	c. 1400	beans and squash reach Huron in Ontario
	1492	Christopher Columbus comes to America
	1497	John Cabot comes to Cape Breton and Newfoundland
	1500s	Spanish bring horses to Mexico. Horses begin to spread northward
	1534	Jacques Cartier claims Atlantic coast region for France
	1604	French begin settling Acadia (Atlantic coast region)
	1608	Champlain starts settlement at Quebec City
	1610	Henry Hudson comes to Hudson Bay
	1611	Membertou, a Micmac chief, becomes first Indian Christian in Canada
	1613	French and British start war in Atlantic coast region
	1615	Huron meet Champlain and Father Le Caron
	1649	Huron forced to abandon villages

1670	Hudson's Bay Company founded
1700s	Métis nation grows in west. Métis work in fur trade
1745	Haida meet Russian traders. Sea otter trade begins
1754	Blackfoot refuse to hunt for Hudson's Bay Company
1759	British defeat French at Quebec
1763	France surrenders Canada to Britain
	Royal Proclamation by Charles II lays basis for aboriginal rights
1776	American Revolution begins
1780s	Six Nations Indians come to Canada
	American loyalist settlers begin to move in large numbers to Canada
1802	Peter Jones born
1821	Hudson's Bay Company and Northwest Company merge. Métis settlers move to Red River
1844	Louis Riel born
1856	Peter Jones dies
1867	Confederation of Canada. *British North America Act* gives federal government jurisdiction over Indians
1869	Hudson's Bay Company surrenders its territory to Canada. Louis Riel sets up provisional government in Red River
1870	First Riel "rebellion" ends. *Manitoba Act* passed
1870s	Buffalo dying out on prairies. European settlers begin moving west
1873	Northwest Mounted Police formed
1871–1921	"Numbered Treaties" signed

1876	Haida acquire first missionary. *Indian Act* passed
1884	*Indian Act* forbids potlatch
1885	Second Riel "rebellion." Riel hanged
	Canadian Pacific Railroad completed
1913	Nishga petition government for recognition of their aboriginal rights
1914–1918	Native people serve in World War I
1923	Last Indian treaty signed
1939	Supreme Court decides Inuit are "Indians"
1939–1945	Native people serve in World War II
1951	Revised *Indian Act* passed. Ban on potlatch lifted
1960	Status Indians get right to vote
1969	White paper on Indian Policy
1968–1971	National Native organizations formed
1973	Nishga land case heard by Supreme Court
1974–1977	Judge Thomas Berger conducts Mackenzie Valley Pipeline Inquiry
1975	James Bay Settlement
1981	Canadian Constitution provides partial recognition of aboriginal rights

Bibliography

The following books are recommended to those who wish to read further about the past, present, and future of Canada's Native people.

For the Beginning Student of Native Studies
Blakely, Phyllis R. *The Micmacs.* Don Mills: Addison-Wesley (Canada), 1974
Coatsworth, Emerson S. *Nomads of the Shield: Ojibwa Indians.* Toronto: Ginn, 1970
Harris, Christie. *Raven's Cry.* New York: Atheneum, 1966.
Jury, Wilfred and Elsie M. Jury. *Sainte-Marie Among the Hurons.* Toronto: Oxford University Press, 1954.
Kidd, Kenneth. *Canadians of Long Ago.* Toronto: Academic Press, 1951.
Campbell, Maria. *Riel's People: How the Métis Lived.* Vancouver: Douglas & McIntyre, 1978.
Teaching Approaches
LaRoque, Emma. *Defeathering the Indian.* Agincourt: The Book Society of Canada, 1975.
Manitoba Indian Brotherhood. *The Shocking Truth about Indians in Textbooks.* Winnipeg: Author, 1974.
McDiarmid, Garnet and David Pratt. *Teaching Prejudice.* Toronto: Ontario Institute for Studies in Education, 1971.

Native Culture: General Surveys
Cox, Bruce (Ed.). *Cultural Ecology: Readings on the Canadian Indians and Eskimos.* Toronto: McClelland and Stewart, 1973.
Spencer, Robert F. and Jesse D. Jennings et al. *The Native Americans: Ethnology and Backgrounds of the North American Indians.* Second Edition. New York: Harper and Row, 1977.

General Reading
Berger, Thomas R. *Northern Frontier, Northern Homeland: The Report of the Mackenzie Valley Pipeline Inquiry, Vol. 1.* Ottawa: Supply and Services, 1977.
Dempsey, Hugh. *Charcoal's World.* Saskatoon: Western Producer Prairie Books, 1978.
Dempsey, Hugh. *Crowfoot: Chief of the Blackfeet.* University of Oklahoma Press, 1972.
Graburn, Nelson H. H. *Eskimos Without Igloos: Social and Economic Development in Sugluk.* Boston: Little, Brown & Co., 1969.
Jones, Peter. (Kahkewaquonaby). *History of the Ojebway Indians.* London: AW Bennett, 1861. (reprint ed., Books For Libraries Press, Freeport, New York, 1970.)
LaViolette, Forrest E. *The Struggle for Survival: Indian Cultures and the Protestant Ethic in British Columbia.* Toronto: University of Toronto Press, 1973.
Martin, Calvin. *Keepers of the Game: Indian-Animal Relationships and the Fur Trade.* Berkeley: University of California Press, 1978.
McFeat, Tom. (Ed.) *Indians of the North Pacific Coast.* Toronto: McClelland and Stewart, 1966.

McGee, H. F. (Ed.) *The Native Peoples of Atlantic Canada: A History of Ethnic Interaction.* Toronto: McClelland and Stewart, 1974.

Patterson, F. Palmer. *The Canadian Indian: A History Since 1500.* Don Mills: Collier Macmillan Canada, 1972.

Quimby, George R. *Indian Life in the Upper Great Lakes.* Chicago: 1960.

Sealey, D. Bruce and Antoine S. Lussier. *The Métis: Canada's Forgotten People.* Winnipeg: Manitoba Métis Federation Press, 1975.

Siggner, Andrew J. *An Overview of Demographic, Social and Economic Conditions among Canada's Registered Indian Population.* Ottawa: Indian and Northern Affairs, 1979.

Smith, Donald B. "The Mississauga, Peter Jones, and the White Man: The Algonkians' Adjustment to the Europeans on the North Shore of Lake Ontario to 1860." Ph.D. thesis, University of Toronto, 1975.

Stanley, George F. G. *Louis Riel.* Toronto: Ryerson Press, 1963.

Trigger, Bruce G. *The Huron: Farmers of the North.* Toronto: Holt, Rinehart, and Winston, 1969.

Valentine, Victor F. and Frank G. Vallee. *Eskimo of the Canadian Arctic.* Toronto: McClelland and Stewart, 1968.

Wallis, Wison D. and Ruth Sawtell Wallis. *The Micmac Indians of Eastern Canada.* Minneapolis: University of Minnesota Press, 1955.

Wiley, Gordon R. *An Introduction to American Archaeology, Vol. 1.* Englewood Cliffs, New Jersey: Prentice-Hall, 1966.

Index

aboriginal title   119–120
Acadia   21–22
"Anicinabe"   52
Arctic region   8, 77
art, Native   126
Asia   3
assimilation, policy of   112–113
Atlantic coast region   7, 13

baskets   17, 23, 25
beans   28–29
Beothuk   6, 13
Berger, Thomas   121
Bering Strait   2–3
Biard, Father   19, 21
birchbark canoes   21, 44
bison, big-horned   2
Blackfoot Indians   51–63
boarding schools   114
bolas   82
British North America Act   118
Buckingham House   61
buffalo   4, 8, 53–54, 56, 94, 113
"buffalo-runners"   57–58, 94

candlefish   67
canoe   6, 16, 44, 67
caribou   82
carrioles   94
Cartier, Jacques   20, 104
cedar   67
China   74
Christianity   21–22, 34, 47, 109
Circumpolar Conference   89
clan   32, 47
Cocking, Mathew   61
Confederation   97
corn   28–31, 43
cornbread recipe   31
corn flour   30
coups   57
coup stick   59
"Credit Chief"   48
Credit reserve   48
Crowfoot   62
culture   5, 86, 91, 97, 118, 123–127

Department of Indian Affairs   112, 114, 118

diet   123
Duck Lake   99

Edenshaw, Charles   72
education   125
eight fires, story of   130
"Elnu"   52
Eskimo   77

fishing   41–42
frostbite   79
fur trade   34–35, 91, 106–107, 110

glaciers   2
Glooscap   18
Great Lakes region   7, 27
Grand Banks   104
Grand Medicine Society   45
Gulf Stream   15

Haida   65–75
harpoon   80–81
harpoon heads   80–81
health   124
Henday, Anthony   61
herbs   45
heritage   124–127
Hochelaga   21
horse racing   94
horses   54, 56–58, 63
housing   123
Hudson, Henry   87
Hudson's Bay Company   61, 88, 95–97, 107
Huron Indians   27–37
Huronia   29, 33–34

Ice Age   2, 15, 54
identity, Native   124–127
igloo   79
Ile Ste. Marie   36
Indian Act   74, 112, 114, 117–118, 128
Indian agents   117
"Indian Policy" paper   128
Inuit   77–89, 117–118
"Inuk"   77
Iroquois   36

James Bay agreement   122
Jesuit "Relations"   37

Jesuits   21–22, 34, 37
jobs, Native   123
Jones, Peter (Kahkewaquonaby)   47–49

kamiks   79
King of France   20
kayak   82

land bridge   2, 4
land rights, Native   97, 111, 119–122
language families   8–11
L'Anse Aux Meadows   104
Le Caron, Joseph   34
lineage   69–70
longhouses   32–33

Mackenzie Valley Pipeline Inquiry   122
mammoth   2
Manitoba Act   98
maple sugar   42
marriage   24–25, 86
martyr   37
matrilineage   69
mede   45
medicine   126
medicine bundle   59
Membertou   21
Methodists   47
Métis   91–101, 117–119
Métis colonies   119
Micmac Indians   13–35
Micmac Calendar   17
Micmac summer festival   18
Midewewin Society   45, 49
Moodie, Susannah   109

Nanabush   1
Native people (definition)   117
Nishga Indian land claims   120
nomads   6
non-status Indians   117–119
Norse   87, 104
northern forest region   6, 39
North West Company   95
Northwest Mounted Police   62–63
numbered treaties   110–113
"Nunavut"   124
nutrients   15

Ojibwa Indians   39–49

Pacific region   8, 65
parka   79, 82

pemmican   54
plankton   15
polar bear   83
Port Royal   21
potlatch   69–70, 74–75
pottery   31–32
Prairie region   7, 51
provisional government (Métis)   97, 99

Queen Charlotte Islands   65, 74

Récollets   34
Red River   96–99
Red River carts   94–95
Red River Jig   93
region (definition of)   5
regions, Canada's   6–8
"Relations"   37
religion, Native   126
reserves   23, 63, 113, 118–119
Riel   97–100
Riel Rebellion(s)   96–101
"roof of the world"   77

sagas, Norse   104
salmon   8, 67
Scott, Thomas   97
seals   80, 86
sharing   83–86
Siberia   77
"Siksika"   52
Six Nations   109
slaves   69
snowshoes   6, 16, 21, 44
spear points   4
spirit helper   58, 60–61
spirits   86
spiritual beliefs, Native   126
squash   28–29
Stadacona   21
status Indians   117–119, 123
Ste. Croix Island   21
Ste. Marie among the Hurons   37
Supreme Court   118

thirteen colonies   109
tipi(s)   8, 55
toboggan   6, 16, 44
totem pole   70, 72–73
trading posts   61, 106
travois   53
treaties   110–113, 118–119

Treaty Number Seven   63
treeline   8
Trudeau, Prime Minister   120
tundra   77

ulu knife   77
umiak   82
unemployment, Native   123

Wabnaki Confederacy   22
War of Independence   109
whales   82, 87
whisky   61–62
wigwam(s)   16, 45
wild rice   42–43, 123

Yoscaha   34

zhagonosh   130